The Cumberland River Review
The First Five Years

To Tayla,

The Chimes looks terrific.

Best of luck with the

writing & travel.

— Graham

The Cumberland River Review
The First Five Years

edited by
Graham Hillard

and
Noula Arroyo, Katerine Avila-Pastor, Katie Dickau,
Torri Frye, Amanda Johnson, Christian Mack, Katie Riddle

Published by *The Cumberland River Review*
Trevecca Nazarene University
333 Murfreesboro Road
Nashville, Tennessee, 37210
All Rights Reserved
http://crr.trevecca.edu

ISBN-13: 978-1981520299
ISBN-10: 1981520295

Cover Art:
"Untitled (193, 184, 141, 109)" by Jane Hammond
1990, oil on linen, 76" x 70"

The Cumberland River Review (ISSN 2326-0009) is a quarterly online publication of new poetry, fiction, essays, and art. The journal is produced by the department of English at Trevecca Nazarene University, in Nashville, Tennessee, and welcomes submissions from both national and international writers and artists.

CONTENTS

Introduction

The statistic is so axiomatic, so obvious a depiction of reality, that it hardly needs sourcing or verification: Most literary magazines fail within their first five years of publication. So why has *The Cumberland River Review* made it this far? Why, furthermore, is there no end in sight for a magazine whose masthead includes no famous names and whose primary virtue—indeed, whose primary aim!— might best be described as a methodical, dogged consistency?

The answer, first and foremost, lies in the skill and generosity of the 181 contributors who have filled our digital pages and the 41 editors (you'll find a list of them in this book's final pages) who have worked on the magazine over the years. So, too, have we benefited from extraordinary institutional support, and the administrative staff of Trevecca Nazarene University, our sponsoring college and academic home, deserve great thanks. Yet I'll give at least modest credit to our vision—defined loosely at our founding and maintained daily by our crack team of editors—of what poetry ought to be. The work in this anthology, and in our quarterly issues, must not be didactic, need not preach or teach, yet neither must it be empty, self-directed. To borrow the categories named by Mark Jarman and Robert McDowell in *The Reaper Essays*, we exclude all "navel-gazers and mannerists."

Does *CRR* risk self-importance (or, worse, self-parody) by insisting on work of moral consequence? The reader will decide. Let him do so, however, only after giving full attention to the often extraordinary contributions aggregated below. Let her read William Logan's masterful examination of what time claims or leaves untouched. Or Lisa Dominguez Abraham's clear-eyed portrayal of parental exhaustion and the minor miracles that sometimes intrude upon it. Or Brian Swann's lovely take on "the old romantic rift between self and world," to quote fellow contributor Ann Lauinger.

Lauinger's astute phrase is merely a sample of what the reader can expect to find within: not only the poems themselves but a long conversation, as poets reflect on what their work has meant to them—as peers consider what it might mean to others. We've taken great delight in assembling such a collection and wish the reader equal joy. In the meantime, we'll be releasing new issues every January, April, July, and October, on the 15th of the month, *esto perpetua*. Here's to the next five years.

-Graham Hillard, Editor
January 2018

William Logan

Venice in the Eighties

We racked over the chop of the lagoon,
bell towers backlit by North African skies,
as if the sirocco had at last blown into Byzantium,
the whole effect staged by some set designer
on Ritalin, the sunset sinking to lapis lazuli
alleys below the gleam of windows newly lit,
the salty perfume almost sheer guile.
Ahead lay those refugees of geometry,
canted towers, palazzi in their desert chalks,
sewery puddles along broken flags.
We stood at the Grand Canal,
the winter residents in *seppie*, as if for funeral mass,
swarming across narrow bridges, stone steps
slicked with ice, a hell cold but infernal.
We passed, I swear, two nuns in Wellingtons.
The waters were so still, those brief dawns,
a counter-Venice rose within, reflected
without ripple or crease. There remained
an unspoken melancholy, each vision
no longer new, the specters crawling
one after another like the ghosts toward Odysseus.
Years before, we had lain beneath the frescoes
of a down-at-heels pensione whose windows
gave onto the roof tiles of a church by Canaletto.
There the Mediterranean lizards convened,
Metternichs of the terra cotta.
Turning through an unknown *calle*,
you wrapped in my llama-brown Zegna,
we lost our way, the winter evening so dark
even the signs refused their meaning.
At last a greater shadow loomed before us.
The Frari proved so much colder than Dante's hell,
a holocaust of Bibles could not have warmed it.

You lingered before Barthel's masterpiece,
the funerary monument of Pésaro—four slaves
bound in ivory rags, eyes whited out,
shouldering the entablature,
its weight in the strained flexure of their arms,
betraying all those Africans galleyed
and ironed in forgotten wars, as if marble
knew the anger of marble. It was an artist's trick,
of course, one of those classical gestures
that make the unbearable bearable.

Yet we stood, unable to return
to our four-star hotel, because we had turned to salt.

William Logan on "Venice in the Eighties"

We first visited the Frari, one of the three great churches in Venice, when an old cowboy friend offered to send us to Italy in search of *fumetti*, Italian pornographic comics—very popular square, thick books, often with supernatural heroines. He didn't care where we started, so long as we ended in Naples, home of the used *fumetti* trade. My sweetheart and I flew to Venice; there, on an evening wander, we first walked into the great barn of that church. The poem begins on a later visit, but it looks back to the first, when Venice still possessed the shock of the new, and the shock of the very old.

Jeanne Murray Walker on "Venice in the Eighties"

No location could be more fitting for a poem of regret than Venice. The center of politics and power in the 14th century, Venice soon fell upon hard times. By the 18th and 19th centuries, it had become little more than the subject of paintings and sketches. Now, as water levels rise, Venice is literally sinking.

In William Logan's "Venice in the Eighties," the narrator and his lover re-visit Venice almost forty years after their first stay. In place of their former charming "down-at-heels pensione," they can book into a four-star hotel. But

Venice is "no longer new" to them. "[C]old but infernal," it arouses "unspoken melancholy." By the end of the poem, like Lot's wife, who looked back, they have turned to salt.

Logan laconically observes in the poem that visual art tricks the viewer and so makes "the unbearable bearable." It's no surprise, then, that his own tricks render the utter desolation of Venice powerful on the one hand and, on the other, mercifully bearable. No paraphrase can do justice to the poem's internal rhyme, flexible iambic pentameter, rich puns, irony, and detailed visual, tactile, and sound images. Just please read the poem again. Experience the despair of the aging couple in Venice. But also enjoy the pleasure of how brilliantly their journey is recounted.

Jeanne Murray Walker

Border Crossing

for Steve Shoemaker

Mid November. The cicada's ardent song
grows deafening. Wind rubs the oak's old joints.
Something's going to happen.
                           The sky goes wrong,
purpling the way it purpled at the checkpoint
that day the border guard pawed through my luggage.
My heart skipped its ragged rope—child
that I became—as he lectured in a language
I didn't understand, then grinned and piled
my books into his bag, and waved me through
without them.
                  That's the kind of line we're about
to cross. You will lay down your precious words,
your name. They won't be any use. You'll
climb the highest pass, wordless. A shout,
a greeting, and
                  the sky's all sudden, golden birds.

Jeanne Murray Walker on "Border Crossing"

I wrote this sonnet for Steve Shoemaker, a guy who befriended me when we were both students at Wheaton College. Steve towered above most of us at 6 feet 8 inches, maybe. A fabulous basketball player, he was very funny, and he also wrote poetry.

I got to know Steve because I edited the campus literary magazine, to which he submitted that poetry. When I met him—in the late 60's—I discovered that he, like me, was a war protester. With other friends, we spent our early twenties bewildered and enraged by the murders of the Kennedys, Martin Luther King, Medgar Evers. Steve went on brilliantly to direct and vastly expand The YMCA in Urbana, Illinois. At his request, I came to do a poetry reading there about ten years ago. That was the last time I saw him.

When he got sick, not knowing what else to offer him, I wrote a sonnet pondering the margin between life and death, the line we both knew he would be crossing soon. I remembered an ominous border I had recently crossed from Austria into Hungary.

Steve crossed his final border in October, 2016.

After writing this sonnet, I went on to draft about a hundred more, many of which will soon be published under the title *Pilgrim, You Find the Path by Walking*.

Chase Twichell on "Border Crossing"

This mysterious little lyric speaks to me on several levels. I love the way the "something" that's "going to happen" stays in the future. The poem speculates about it—"the kind of line we're about / to cross"—but doesn't make it explicit, though it's likened to something as scary and wrong as theft by a border guard in a foreign country. By embedding the remembered incident in the middle of the prediction, the poem makes us understand how deeply the speaker's heart is threatened without requiring us to know anything about the relationship that's apparently about to end. The surprise is that the sky, which "goes wrong" earlier in the poem, ends as "sudden, golden birds," a suggestion that there may be relief as well as sadness and fear in the crossing-over.

Chase Twichell

The Missing *Weekly Readers*

One Sunday noon at 436
(Gram's house—the entire family
referred to their houses

by street number—),
the first big snow was falling.
We sat around the table

in an igloo: the dining room
darkened and hushed,
windows a swollen glow.

After lunch, the cousins
split up to play. Sam and I
roamed the neighborhood,

feral kids invisible
behind the schoolyard's
white chenille chain link.

We looted the small covered
bridge of the mailbox with great care,
disturbing no snow.

Only Sam and I know where
the *Weekly Readers* for the week
of February 16th, 1958, reside.

If you find, in a surprising place,
a note left by kids sixty years ago,
you'll understand why

the kids' gesture moves me.
Behind it is an impulse
to touch a stranger.

Chase Twichell on "The Missing Weekly Readers*"*

When I was a kid, we often had big Sunday lunches at my grandmother's house, formal affairs during which the various undertows of adult life were revealed if you paid attention. No raised voices ever, but always the subtle rancor and chafing of long marriages and profound political and philosophical differences. The poem tells a true story—my cousin Sam's and my theft and concealment of the third grade *Weekly Readers* from the nearby school mailbox. I often wonder if the people who bought my grandmother's house after she died ever found them, or what they thought of the note we left, which I would love to read now. I think we stole them to make an unconscious pact, like blood-siblings, of solidarity against forces that seemed to us both dangerous and unchangeable.

Kerry James Evans on "The Missing Weekly Readers*"*

When I think of snow, I think of concealment—a cold blanket to protect a scarred, vulnerable patch of earth until the sun, once again, assumes its throne. The trope of snow is not a new one, but in this poem it works so well with memory and place, with the genuine hope to connect with another: not only in the moment, but once the snow thaws, as it does in the recollection of this memory—not only by the speaker, but by the reader, who is indeed as much of a character as one of the "feral kids" from the poem. I love how the poem acts as a web spanning sixty years of time, space, characters, and seasons, and how, in the end, the children in the poem remind us of the importance of discovery—that so long as we are seeking, nothing remains invisible forever, and that we are never truly "missing."

Kerry James Evans

Iron City

There, beside the cotton gin,
squats the fattest turkey buzzard in Georgia,
one wing either broken or certain,
elbow bent like our world
before logic descended from heaven
on a fiery cloud: fire that the ancients
deified with monuments—
triangles raised upon squares
in valleys where the dead
still rise when the river swells.
Fire that the welder masters with a torch,
fashioning entire cities of iron,
the fields around him still raw
from the picking, railroads
strung like licorice over a fallen ladder.
The tracks hardly rattle a word.
Poison sumac blushes while a tractor
pulls a plow through clay, and that
—that hammer you just heard?
That was an anvil giving way.

Kerry James Evans on "Iron City"

More and more, the structures of what hold a place together, or hold an
identity, whether societal or individual, seem to be in flux. This has probably
always been true, but the anxiety of living in a world that emphasizes our
loneliness, our confusion about who and where we are, seems to highlight just
how in the dark we are. All we really know for sure? We don't know where
we're headed. We're following an extremely crazed yet generous star around a
black hole. We're stardust being flushed down a toilet, and I think this poem
is waking up—as many of us are—to this sobering truth. "The anvil giving
way" is our ego—our desire to control a world that would never exist without

us. I think whether we want to or not, we—as a planet—are beginning to let go of what we think we know.

Richard Luftig on "Iron City"

"Iron City" represents everything I love in a poem. It is geographical, accessible, and highly imagistic. Kerry James Evans has created a mysterious universe, one we might see in an Edward Hopper painting. There were people there once; in fact, the place was vibrant and busy. There seem to be people there now, but they are unseen, out of the picture's edge. Meanwhile, everything that we *do* see—old barns, rusting rails, the fat buzzard—has experienced better days. "Iron City" reminds me of the Midwestern poet Ted Kooser—such a comparison is, I believe, high praise. It is a poem that any reader, even those typically "turned off" by poetry, can read, appreciate, and relate to.

Richard Luftig

On a Lake in Indiana

This cabin does not wear its winters well
but rather like threadbare clothes pressed too close
against the skin. Its steps are hidden
beneath a pyramid of leaves as if
awaiting some long past owner who might
yet arrive. On the front porch, wishes stacked
like cordwood now reduced to kindling wait
for the opportunity to move inside,
and Adirondack chairs are still saving seats
in the hope that someone might return.

The wood all around the wind-leaked windows
is gray and flaked, while in the fireplace
dead ashes strew themselves with each opening
and slamming of the doors. You can run
your hands over the sinew of knotted
wall boards, feel the faint pulse from when the place
was new. On top of the mantel, I find

a corncob pipe still filled with tobacco
and trace my finger over the rough bowl
like a blind man reading a stranger's face,
searching for a sign, some hint, some proof
of the people who have dreamed here before.

The Editors on "On a Lake in Indiana"

Rereading "On a Lake in Indiana," I find myself returning to the compelling
description of the front porch. The personification Luftig employs there—the
"kindling wait[ing] / for the opportunity to move inside"; the "Adirondack
chairs . . . still saving seats / in the hope that someone might return"—reveals
just how abandoned the place is. The narrator, one almost feels, is both

present and absent, and one senses that the loneliness of the cabin cannot be disturbed either way. I'm reminded of my great aunt's old cabin in upstate New York. She built a newer cabin next to it many years before I was born, yet I always found myself going back to the old one. I could spend hours roaming its grounds, searching every room, and listening to my grandmother's stories of when that place was itself new. I believe that that cabin's "knotted / wall boards" and "wind-leaked windows" told their own stories, just as Luftig's do. (-*Katie Dickau*)

Ricardo Pau-Llosa

Priam

for Ismael Gómez Peralta, painter of Havana in ruins

Let not my son be remembered in any
stubborn way that wields or any ardor
that befalls. Let no trumpet
or banner like the sun signal him in strange

recollection. Instead, let the stories range
at will, distort his cunning and intent
that his image might become, like armor,
a shifting shell that meets whatever need.

In this veiling way, let his people
always be those who turn the molten
streets into paths a journey must understand.
Not those who rail but those who sigh and ripple

and so conjure fugues more lunatic than war
and live as rebels singing orders to order.

Matthew Minicucci on "Priam"

Though the term "painterly" is tossed about quite a bit when it comes to
poets and poetry, I do consider it apropos to Ricardo Pau-Llosa's poem
"Priam," perhaps most of all when one is considering the concept of
composition. When the term "fugues" appears in the penultimate line, so
much seems to become clear: the voices and intonations repeating their
pitches along the centuries; Priam, that great king of Troy, a man who begged
for the body of his own son. The brief dedication to Ismael Gomez Peralta
creates a feeling almost chiastic: this repeating, this crossing over and over at
will, some composer's fugue hidden in the support beams of a long-
weathered house that still stands, despite everything that's come before and

everything to follow. We repeat ourselves, Pau-Llosa's speaker reminds us, and people will say what they will. "Let not my son be remembered" is a statement in opposition to what Hector himself says to his own son, despite what he knows (what we know) will happen when Troy falls. Troy is always falling, Pau-Llosa reminds us; the ruins are just outside this window, in such beautiful blues and nearly impossible golds.

Matthew Minicucci

Paul's Letter to the Corinthians (2)

There's a reason Greek has a vocative case: any thorn in flesh you can find; rocks pitted against high tide. You decide, then mind the pits, poison, or bitter taste of the olive's uncured flesh. A metaphor, perhaps, and to be expected, or expunged depending on the context. It's not that fruit isn't possible at this moment, it's just unlikely. Perhaps winter. Perhaps a blight of unknown origins: pathogenic organism; the blind white chlorosis of fungi. I don't mean to explain these things. I stand only as a farmer of men. My path took roads with no soil to speak of, so I leave this tree with you. My chains keep me here, rooted, a moment blind. Forgive this crude hand. It speaks only in looped alphas, or alephs—if we must—which always seem to find the day's last, silent light.

Matthew Minicucci on "Paul's Letter to the Corinthians (2)"

This poem appears in my second book, *Small Gods*, along with a poem for (nearly) every Pauline epistle. The hope with this poem (and the project in general) was not only to capture specific language and images from the letters themselves but to be considerate of Paul, who writes, in many ways, outside of what each recipient thinks faith is supposed to be. My speaker, in the same way, is trying to understand faith. For this particular epistle, I'm concentrating on the dichotomy of pain and faith, and also the reproach Paul is responding to in 2nd Corinthians. Part of the path of the poem is this slow disintegration of the physical, as evidenced by its "blight" and "pathogen." Even more, I was left thinking about the disintegration of the physical Paul himself: mostly blind at the end of his life, apologizing in text for the quality of his handwriting. For whatever reason, this image sticks with me: that the disintegration of self might be inexorably connected to our inevitable step into that next world.

There is awfully little verse in the New Testament, but the Pauline epistles are chock full of poetry. Paul's facility with paradox ("Has not God made foolish the wisdom of the world?" —1 Cor. 1:20) lies at the heart of these letters, as does his talent for metaphor. Both strategies reject literal fact for the mystery of spiritual insight.

In his second letter to the church in Corinth, Paul is at his most vulnerable. Much of the book is spent defending his ministry from critics, and, in chapter 12, we find the metaphor that Minicucci takes up at the opening of this poem: "the thorn in the flesh." Paul has asked God to spare him from some unnamed source of suffering ("Perhaps winter. Perhaps a blight of unknown origins . . . ."), but God has denied his request via paradox: "My power is made perfect in weakness" (2 Cor. 12:9). The speaker of Minicucci's poem, Paul or some contemporary inheritor of Paul's metaphors, responds to that paradox with one of his own: Though he is unable to taste the fruit's sweetness, he brings that sweetness to others ("I leave this tree with you"). Further, his suffering (his thorn, his chain) not only causes him pain but paradoxically "roots" him, turns him into the fruit tree. The blight is a blessing. Like the Biblical letter from which it is drawn, Minicucci's poem showcases exactly what poetry is capable of: the imaginative recapitulation of reality into something truer.

George David Clark

Gardensong

in the gardens
        in the gardens
you are walking
        you are walking
through the roses
        to the roses

you are almost
        you are talking
in a whisper
        like a whisper
to the roses
        mottled roses

now you're leaving
        now you're leaving
through the tulips
        through the tulips
night is falling
        lightly falling

bye to you
        goodbye to you
by the pansies
        'side the pansies
by the pansies
        bye to you

George David Clark on "Gardensong"

I'd been reading Robert Hass's essay "Listening and Making," which includes
a passage from Nils Petersen: "Whereas in silks / Whereas in silks / My Julia

goes / My Julia goes / Then, then, methinks (methinks) / How sweetly flows / Sweetly flows / The liquefaction (faction) (faction) / Of her clothes / her clothes her clothes." I loved the playfulness of Petersen's lyric, and I found myself thinking about the ways in which echoes might intensify a statement even as the volume fades. Ultimately, I wondered what I might be able achieve in a poem that radically limited its vocabulary and imagery to pursue meaning largely through repetition and rhythm.

At the time, I lived just up the street from a garden park in Valparaiso, Indiana. Here, I seem to be imagining something of a missed connection set among those flowers. If the poem works as I intend, maybe we hear the echoes of a romantic overture this speaker never quite summons the courage to assert.

Shane Seely on "Gardensong"

I read "Gardensong" and hear two singers in close harmony, sometimes producing direct echoes, and other times—times when my hair stands up a little—bending the call in the response, as in "to the roses / mottled roses." That mottling, of course, suggests the sense of loss, both sudden and gradual, that haunts this poem: Through the garden full of roses and tulips and pansies, through the "lightly falling" night, someone is leaving. The singers' notes are as mournful as they are warm, and the footfall of the person leaving is almost imperceptible. Yet this speaker is so acutely aware of the loss as it is happening—and it is happening so quietly, almost tenderly—that no breath can be admitted.

Shane Seely

Lost Ring

My finger drawn thin in the cold sun
of late December, the ring slid
insensibly somewhere into nowhere,
invisible among the understuff
like a gnome's treasure. The first sign
was the sensation of the raw air
around the little band of skin
the ring had rested on. Had it
fallen in the leaves I'd left
unraked about the yard, now sogged
into a mat between the tufts of grass?
Had it flown off when I threw
into the weedy edge the dregs
I'd dredged from the birdbath's
almost-ice? Had it rolled among
the dead stalks of the asters left
unpruned? So much goes overgrown
if not attended to. I keep
imagining its glint against
the lowered sun, its silver O
not quite the O it was
before the world reforged it. And the line
inscribed on its inside face, gone
inscrutable beyond the threshold
of the read world. The sun
stubs itself against the trees.
Here's my hand, un-
inscribed, empty as the ring now lost
to the history of dirt, now remembered
by the small weight of its absence.

Shane Seely on "Lost Ring"

I first knew that I had lost the ring my wife had given me, lost it somewhere in the wet, cold, overgrown yard of our first home, when I suddenly felt around the finger that had worn the ring a sharp band of cold. I looked down and saw instead of the silver ring a ring of paler skin, skin that hadn't seen sun in the years I'd worn the ring on it. How present the ring was to me then. I searched and searched, sure its silver surface would stand out in the gray-green of my winter yard, but I never found the thing. It struck me then that all the things the ring had meant—as a gift, as a reminder of my love's presence, as a vessel for a lovely sentiment—it only meant because I wore it. In the weeds it couldn't mean anything at all.

Eleanor Kedney on "Lost Ring"

Shane Seely immediately puts the reader into a scene with a narrator who has lost an intimate object—a ring. The description of the sun as "cold" and of the ring as sliding "insensibly" into "nowhere," becoming "invisible," creates a mood of loss, as well as the feeling that the ring is gone forever. We're not told if the band is a wedding ring, and it's described only by the sensation of "raw air" on the skin where it once "rested." I love this restraint on Seely's part; it allows the reader to supply his or her own emotions about the metaphor of the lost ring. We learn a lot about the narrator's world in the descriptions of where the ring may have fallen. The yard is "unraked," the edges "weedy," and the unpruned asters "dead stalks." The turn in the poem comes in the lines "so much goes overgrown / if not attended to," suggesting that the narrator is talking about much more than a neglected yard. I find it heartbreaking that the narrator keeps imagining the ring's "glint"—a flash of light—despite the ring's having been changed by the world, its inscription gone. The longing to find it again comes through. I love the active image of the sun that "stubs itself against the trees," while the narrator's hand is compared to the ring: uninscribed, empty, and lost. Any readers who have lost something or someone dear to them will find Seely's poem moving. That's all of us.

Eleanor Kedney

Reading Frank O'Hara After My Mother's Death

I buy an *Arizona Daily Star* to read obituaries
in which everyone was kind, generous, and will be missed.
The advice given from a heart doctor:
"Don't look at the stat monitors;
you can't live by the numbers."
There were days hers were so good.
This month, a blue moon on New Year's Eve.
The maid at the Waldorf, a Russian Jew, told me,
get out and walk. "Don't look at anybody,
don't go into stores, just walk."
In St. Bartholomew's church,
a woman turned to a man—
"God wants you to live as long as possible."
I just wanted quiet.
The kind of quiet that comes out of stillness:
hummingbird wings sculling the air;
Ave Maria sung as liturgy by an opera singer.
I took a wrong turn today up the mountain.
Now, I wear blue topaz, the color of my mother's eyes.
Oval stones in a bracelet, hoop earrings.
Though I am not mineral or vitreous
I have been touched, turned, warmed, and cut.
I want to believe that the dog lick-kisses my lips
because she loves me and not
for the sweet jam in the corners of my mouth.
Now, I count lights when I drive,
snack instead of eat meals.
Now, the wave of a bare greasewood in the wind,
the orange flowers that hang on
the Cape honeysuckle in January amaze me.

During the time my mother was in the hospital, I wasn't writing. After she died, I wanted to start again. I was grieving, and I knew that I couldn't write about my feelings head-on, narratively. I needed distance and freedom. My world had changed, but the world around me had not. It was very painful to go anywhere. I started reading Frank O'Hara's *Selected Poems*. O'Hara made his interactions with the day-to-day world, and his sensitive response to it, his subjects. His use of matter-of-fact speech, combined with intimate proclamations, allowed his speakers' vulnerability to come through in his poems. This was very helpful in my own establishing of a narrator, giving me the distance I was looking for. O'Hara's style inspired me to try his techniques. Stressing voice, listing specific details of everyday life after my mother's death, and contrasting images allowed me to express my grief. The poem became titled "Reading Frank O'Hara After My Mother's Death" to acknowledge both his influence and the importance of reading other writers' work, especially when we are struggling to write. I return to this poem for comfort; it helped me through great pain. I also return to it as one that contributed to the evolution of my writing toward a blend of the narrative and the lyric. I'm grateful for Frank O'Hara's poetry for giving me a way to reconnect with the world and express myself when I most needed to do so.

Meg Freitag on "Reading Frank O'Hara After My Mother's Death"

What I love most about this poem is the way it pivots—again and again, to the extent that it's almost playful—while simultaneously managing to keep its raw emotional material suspended in perpetual view. Eleanor Kedney's "Reading Frank O'Hara After My Mother's Death" is, simply put, a study on how grief makes the world suddenly new. The speaker of this poem is simultaneously seeking and listless, and she moves through the world of the poem encountering her everyday experiences as if for the first time. The blue moon on New Year's Eve, blue topaz jewelry, taking a wrong turn in the mountains, a dog licking jam from the corners of the speaker's mouth, honeysuckle in January: This series of disparate images moves us closer to the speaker's grief and allows the understated beauty of what often goes unnoticed to be that much more tender and transcendent. I love the poem's careful music, its linguistic intentionality, and the place of stillness the speaker explicitly calls forth at the very center of the poem—a place in which to quietly reflect for a moment on the lush muck of life that the poem insists on.

Meg Freitag

Ghost of the Lowbush

When time reclaims a landscape, it takes
With it all evidence that something once lived
There. I remember the blueberry fields
Blackening, a black dog running toward me

With a bird's heart in her mouth. I remember
Mosquitoes biting me through my jeans, my watch
Stopping just before midnight. The night
Edith died I felt like one of those ghosts

That doesn't realize it's a ghost
Until the train doesn't hit them, instead
It moves through them. Then they realize
They can't remember the last time

They had a drink of water, or tried to go home.
I walked around my house dying
To touch my forehead to a cool pane of glass.
But every time I'd try it, my face would end up

On the other side, covered in night.
Loving something that's dead isn't the same thing
As dying, but it isn't like being alive, either.
Perhaps it's a case of too much life. How,

In that dream I kept having, the sun was so bright!
It turned everything the same three colors
Until we couldn't tell ourselves apart
From one another. I don't want to forget this feeling

Because when I do, it will mean
She's all the way gone. When he moved away
I carried a letter from him around in my back pocket.
Eventually the words all rubbed off and what remained

Was a soft, fragile square. Then I stopped
Remembering what it had even said and I grieved for him
A second time. On my back in the front lawn, I wept
Loudly into the air, hoping that if maybe

I made it feel something strong enough, the air
Would let me reach back through its masslessness
Into another time—perhaps it would let me touch
My own self's younger shoulder

Where she once sat, straddling, in a blue
Sundress, the crux of his barn roof. And the three of us
Would watch the sky turn the color of malt liquor
As the farmers set their fields on fire.

Meg Freitag on "Ghost of the Lowbush"

This poem is excerpted from my first book, *Edith*, which is a collection of
elegies and apostrophic poems about a beloved pet bird that dies an untimely
death. It is within this thematic constraint that the speaker is able to invoke
other forms of loss, including the dissolution of an important romantic
relationship and the erosion of memory—both of which make an appearance
in this piece.

When we are acutely grieving, we feel a visceral connection to what we have
lost. Often, it can feel like we're losing the thing all over again as the intensity
of the feeling naturally begins to dim. This poem explores the desperate
impulse to cling to our grief, despite how painful it might be. "Ghost of the
Lowbush" is a duel elegy: for Edith, but also for grief itself.

Karen J. Weyant on "Ghost of the Lowbush"

From the first stanza, the reader realizes that Meg Freitag's poem "Ghost of the Lowbush" is very much haunted. We are introduced to a lonely landscape, where the narrator wanders through lonely fields, and where a black dog, "with a bird's heart in her mouth," greets her. We soon learn that that bird, Edith, has died and that a human friend has left, as well, leaving the narrator to explain that that friend's letter has worn into "a soft, fragile square" with the words "all rubbed off."

In essence, there are many ghosts in this poem: the ghost of a landscape, the ghost of a dead loved one, the ghost of someone who has moved or moved on, and the figure of the narrator herself, who feels "like one of those ghosts // That doesn't realize it's a ghost." But most poignant is the ghost of the past, a past for whose sake the narrator mourns for her younger self and happier times, in which "the three of us / Would watch the sky turn the color of malt liquor."

Freitag's quiet hush of a poem is a work of soft tones and images, of whispers and quiet murmurs, of language so precise and lyrical that a reader will have no problem with the presence of ghosts.

Karen J. Weyant

To the Girl Who Can Hear the River Talk

You were born the year of a sudden spring melt,
of a heavy rain that pulled the river from its banks.

Your mother, seven months pregnant with you,
waded through water up to her thighs, wrestled

with garden ornaments and the bicycle your brother
left out on the front lawn overnight.

Even then, you protested by kicking, your tiny feet
doing more pounding than fluttering.

Now, you smell flood waters before the waves swell:
faint sulfur mixed with the moist dirt of a new garden.

You hear the water before it spills, before it rushes
towards West Main, lifting up swings at the park,

tossing around toy buckets in backyard sandboxes,
washing through the first floors of homes

and soaking carpets and furniture, leaving dark puddles
and debris in all the cracks and corners.

You know the river is angry, even before the water swirls
around the old trucks in Old Sam Johnson's backyard,

before it floods Suzy's Bar & Grill, slurping at floorboards
and barstools and torn screens in the doors.

While everyone else listens to the rage after the water rolls
well above flood stage, you can hear how the river

quietly curses before it crests, its muted voice,
Enough, enough, enough, a whisper in the air.

Karen J. Weyant on "To the Girl Who Can Hear the River Talk"

"To the Girl Who Can Hear the River Talk" is partly autobiographical. Like
the "you" in the poem, I was born the year of a flood that did major damage
to my birthplace of Ridgway, a small river town in northern Pennsylvania. My
mother was pregnant with me as she waded through the flood.
These images are really the only facts of the poem, however. From stanza five
until the end of the poem, the "you" is an imaginary character. This character
has surreal powers and can understand the feelings of water. Since I still live
in a river town in northern Pennsylvania, I like to imagine what it would feel
like to really understand the emotion of a flood. The use of second-person
point of view permitted me this surreal vision.

Lisa Dominguez Abraham on "To the Girl Who Can Hear the River Talk"

Karen Weyant's poem moves the way the river moves, deceptively. Her clean
language and musicality are the surface beauty that lures the reader into the
"sudden spring melt / of a heavy rain" and the sensations of a mother who
"wade[s] through water up to her thighs." Then the poem pulls us into the
flood itself. Images gather both momentum and menace, from the scent of
"faint sulfur" to the "dark puddles / and debris in all the cracks and corners"
of people's homes, sweeping us through a remarkably specific town until we
can actually hear the river "slurping at floorboards / and barstools."

The poem ends wonderfully, on curses. Every reader has felt like this river.
And most of us have felt, too, like the girl who senses impending flood. The
final lines evoke Stephen Crane's short story "The Open Boat" when, after a
shipwreck, the survivors "felt that they could then be interpreters" of the sea.
Through Weyant's insights, readers become, with the girl, interpreters of the
river in a way that feels at once authentic, timely, and primal.

Lisa Dominguez Abraham

Christmas Concert

The parents enter exhausted, ears ringing
with the evening commute, with radio news

of bombs in Kabul and campus gunfire
one town over. Even among sparkly cardboard bells

each thinks ahead to a fast food dinner
one more damn time, then bills, then laundry.

Then the curtain stutters open. A third-grader
runs to the piano, arches his hands and plays

Pachelbel's canon in D, notes chosen over 300 years ago
still true. The adults shift and raise eyebrows—

surprisingly good—he's like their own kids, noticed
mostly in fed-up swats and after-bath cuddle.

When, in his short years, did he learn
to wait as end note fades into prayer?

Next, a chubby, messy girl walks onstage.
Mid-December, she wears navy-blue shorts

bunched at the crotch and stares at some back corner
to focus, to project her voice in tones so pure

adult smirks freeze. Somewhere outside
the stars are brightly shining

and the audience holds still, listening
as though she sings a nearly forgotten secret,

as though she herself is the winter secret
whose breath exhales promise.

Lisa Dominguez Abraham on "Christmas Concert"

Parenting challenged me to reenter an elementary school maze in which many
of the adults seemed Other, especially those who were serious about shoebox
panoramas or holiday presentations. But I was grateful to them and still am.
Dedicated grown-ups are the village that ensures human understanding gets
passed along. Thanks to them, I realized that, in learning familiar songs,
children absorb not only cultural motifs but also the core truths within those
shells.

Writing is usually a slow, difficult process for me, but with this poem, for
once, I trusted the center of my own experience. Free verse couplets allowed
me to slow the pace and focus on a theme, common to many faiths, that has
always intrigued me: The holy often appears in disguise. The trick was to not
stray into a list of contemporary horrors or get distracted by the adults.
Instead, I tried to create a path to a girl who is overlooked, like many kids
who lack outward charm, and to recreate for myself the sensation of hearing
truth through her voice.

Patricia L. Hamilton on "Christmas Concert"

I love how "Christmas Concert" lulls us into accepting the parents' point of
view: their world-weariness, their just-trying-to-keep-food-on-the-table
rectitude, their poverty of spirit, even their smugness. Toughing it out day
after day, responsible but beleaguered, they can recognize beauty when it
blossoms unexpectedly before them—Pachelbel's canon in D played
movingly by a third-grader, for instance—but they're slogging through life
with low expectations.

Then *that* child—"a chubby, messy girl"—walks onstage to perform, inadequately dressed in shorts "bunched at the crotch," and for an instant you can imagine the parents' self-vindication: *At least my child . . .* is warmly dressed. Combs her hair. Doesn't eat potato chips all day. *Is loved.* But the "adult smirks freeze"—masterful phrasing, the turning point of the poem— when the unlikeliest source of beauty or grace or truth in the room starts singing "in tones so pure" that the enthralled audience is transported back to that holy night when stars were "brightly shining" and angels proclaimed Christ's incarnation to the shepherds, the unlikeliest of audiences. The girl embodies divine mystery, fusing the roles of angel, prophet, and messiah, all of whose *ruach*—whose breath or spirit— "exhales promise."

Patricia L. Hamilton

Using Chopsticks

That summer we had to pluck quickly
with our chopsticks at whatever spun past—
fried dumplings, buns with savory filling—
if we didn't want to spend the stifling nights
hearing our stomachs growl a bass line
to the high, unearthly hum of cicadas
intoning their ceaseless prayers for rain.

Breakfast brought relief: smooth porcelain
spoons for our bowls of thin rice gruel.
By noon we were starving for Lau Fan's
green beans seasoned with pungent garlic,
for the slivers of chicken that clung to bones
split by sharp cleavers. Chunks and cubes
were easiest to pinch—but we had to grab fast.

We learned to swallow our finicky questions,
not looking too closely at lumps of meat
swimming in shallow pools of grease.
Drenched with the day's heat,
flushed from fiery noodles and boiling broths,
we welcomed wedges of juicy watermelon,
spitting the flat black seeds onto the filthy floor.

Once, Lau Fan brought us a platter heaped
with half-cobs of corn, shucked and boiled.
"Hog feed," the translator assigned to us muttered.
But we cheered and hooted our hero,
who flashed us a gummy, broken-toothed grin.
The next day, he produced a new dish to please us:
thick, crisp Chinese potato chips.

Still, as we roved through shops on our afternoons off,
hoping to chance across cans of lukewarm Coke,
certain longings surfaced—for milkshakes and Big Macs;
sweet red apples; fresh, leafy lettuce.
In our classrooms we pinned up pictures
from magazines we'd brought, printing new words
on the blackboard: bacon, orange juice, raisins, sandwich.

Evenings I savored the tomatoes and cucumbers
Lau Fan peeled for the foreigners, our only raw fare.
As the Lazy Susan whirled, I'd picture my mother
making a salad, the bounty of my father's garden
mounded on her kitchen counter. Gripping my chopsticks
I'd chase the translucent slices, trying to latch onto them—
so tempting, so slippery, like memories of home.

Patricia L. Hamilton on "Using Chopsticks"

I spent the summer of 1985 in Chengdu, Sichuan Province, teaching English
to middle school teachers. China was still a third-world country, one that had
been closed to Westerners for over three decades. Although our team had
excellent training before we left, nothing could adequately prepare us for the
cultural and political differences we encountered. Quickly, I realized that food
is a defining feature of culture—and Sichuanese food was nothing like
Chinese food in America. Years later, focusing on food seemed the best way
to embody the experience in writing. Not only did we have to learn to eat
new foods—such as sea slug, which I cagily managed to avoid—but also we
had to master a completely new physical way of accessing our food. During
our last meal, I remember feeling triumphant upon finally snatching a slippery
tomato slice from the whirling Lazy Susan without dropping it!

Melissa Dickson on "Using Chopsticks"

As a metaphor, using chopsticks represents more than the ordinary task of
eating with a new tool; it stands, too, for the extraordinary task of entering
another culture, of employing one's dexterity and one's tongue in existential

travel. It occurs to me that memory, too, is an existential travel—if existential means "having being in time and space," as good old Mr. Webster claims. I stake my claim, then, that Patricia Hamilton's poem "Using Chopsticks" serves as a time scoop (to borrow a P.K. Dick notion). The imagined chopsticks in the reader's mind grant entry to another place, another time, and another consciousness that is itself in three places and three times: the present of the poem's speaker and her remembered past with its own remembered past. When we are in the poem, we are in Hamilton's longing for the familiar "bounty of my father's garden." We are the growling belly and the "ceaseless prayers." Under the sonic spell of her carefully crafted lines (full of "uuu" and "ooo" and "sss"), the rhythm of her seven septets, and the startling images of the poem's known and unknown foods, we know what Hamilton knows: that the Lazy Susan spins more swiftly than we realize, and we must "grab fast" in the "slippery" and "translucent" moments of becoming.

Melissa Dickson

My Son, Dancing

The last thing I expected, a boy, 10, outside the glass doors
of the ballet studio mirroring each plié and entrechat, his face

as studious as an engineer's confounded by fulcrums and levers.
At home that evening he learned the five elemental positions

from his little sister, and the next week joined her class, the only boy
and nearly a foot taller than the oldest girl. And so I was the mother
    of two

aspiring ballerinas, one in basketball shorts and a pair of borrowed
    shoes,
the other in pigtails, purple chiffon and a pink leotard. What could I
    do

but peer through the glass as the weeks passed and his leaps grew
more graceful, his relevés taller, sturdier, his arms as elegant

as the curves of a silversmith's prize kettle? That he would pirouette
was inevitable, that he would twist his body into improbable
    positions,

lean into the splits the way most boys lean into a pitch, bewildering.
But it was the girls, tiny and shuffling around him, girls

who would soon leap into his steadied arms, that steeled
me for the afternoon he would fall and fail, for a heart's beat, to rise.

Melissa Dickson on "My Son, Dancing"

Perhaps instead of reflecting on the moment that triggered this poem, I will confess the fiction and the emotional truth of it. The boy did not dance long, and, while he had the desire, he didn't have the discipline or the disciplinarian parents to become the dancer I imagined in the poem. He does, however, have the capacity to lose himself in art and music. He does have a broken heart that calls him to create and to imagine. I watch him now practicing guitar and piano in the same random, troubled way that I once practiced drawing. I watch him composing songs that often get abandoned when his skill leaps past that earlier vision. I watch him writing flash-fiction gothic horror stories and speculating on the nature of existence. We bought him a razor last year, and he's on his second skateboard. He makes necklaces out of copper wire and discarded metal bits he finds on the roadside. He sings in the school chorus and dyed his hair Prussian blue. I am still that mother on the other side of the glass, wondering what will become of her baby. I still hope he'll dance.

Kevin L. Cole on "My Son, Dancing"

You don't have to have children in ballet lessons to appreciate "My Son, Dancing." But because I do—one girl and two boys—I was immediately drawn to this poem in which we watch a young boy in ballet lessons. For years, I've tried to write a well-executed poem about watching my children in ballet class but have always fallen short. Dickson's poem achieves what I've always aimed for. Like Degas' paintings of ballerinas and ballet studios, "My Son, Dancing" transports us into the intimate space of the studio, as well as the intimate space of the parent's perceptions as she observes, in poetic wonder, the beauty of children practicing various positions. Again, like Degas, the speaker homes in on a central figure, her son, who, clad in basketball shorts, has traded in sneakers for borrowed ballet shoes. He is disarmingly at ease on the ballet floor, achieving greater grace, dexterity, and mastery with each lesson—a dexterity and grace matched by Dickson's elegant similes. At its conclusion, the poem moves from the particular to the universal, when the speaker says that she must steel herself for "the afternoon he would fall and fail, for a heart's beat, to rise."

Kevin L. Cole

Drought

In the ravine that cleaves two meadows I found
The bone house.
Femurs, spines, a split skull, rib cage, half an antler spread.
Some scattered haphazard
By scavengers, some shaped like nautiluses
By the sluggish shove of last spring's retreating snow.

I have walked this ravine a thousand times,
Never seeing the bones or feeling them under my feet.
But now the thick buffalo grass, the skin of the ravine,
Is diminutive and sere, as brittle and pale as the bones themselves:
It is the season for the grass to concede,
To reveal the secret—where the deer come to die.

I return home in the mid-afternoon, a medieval pilgrim with relics
Walking the border between meadow and corn.
Against the sapphire sky a waxing crescent moon,
Underneath the moon, a thin thread of crows flying low
In single file like a somber jury that must deliver its verdict.
Flushed from my shoes, grasshoppers rattle against husk and leaf.

Just when I think I myself will concede to the judgment
Of the crows, two deer, a doe and four-point in felt,
Bound out of the corn. They pause and stare at me,
Me with my reliquary of winter's bones and they
With their shanks brushing up against
Cup plant and blazing star, rising with furor out of a burned earth.

Kevin L. Cole on "Drought"

I grew up in rural South Texas, which means I grew up with drought and the
relentless fear of drought, a fear that's part of my DNA. And even though

I'm now fifty and live in the Northern Great Plains, nothing has blunted this fear. As poets are like to do, I often confront my fears and unsettled psyche by writing poetry—in this case, a poem set during a severe drought and inspired by a walk on a 350-acre public wildlife preserve, which has been the inspiration for many of my poems. On the one hand, the poem quite simply describes the "events" of that walk. On the other, completing the poem took me three months. I wanted the poem to convey—without being overbearing or trite—the religious, redemptive experience of juxtaposition: the juxtaposition of the chaffed, burned out land against the native flowers and the two deer, startlingly alive, despite the drought.

Scott T. Hutchison on "Drought"

Kevin Cole's "Drought" pays fine, quiet obeisance to earth and sky and animal. The narrator has discovered a final resting place for deer, and the natural world watches this human as he proceeds home, relics in hand, bone dust underfoot. Whatever vague thoughts or designs he may have had in mind for femur and antler, his vision sharpens as he discovers that he is a pilgrim, forced to acknowledge the passage and cycle and place where he walks. The holiness of the scene presses in upon him: seasons transitioning, the sharp vigilant eyes of nature, a waxing moon, the brimming energy of emerging deer. It is a world of flowers blooming, earth eroding, life rising and falling like breath. What has the drought revealed to the narrator? A place we have all walked "a thousand times"—a humbling, worshipful place that exists most often just outside our peripheral vision. Still, it is a place we all know, deep down in our own bones.

Scott T. Hutchison

Hornet's Nest

You sneak in, hit the hornet's nest
with a manly shot of toxins
from ten feet away—then run.
The ball turret hole
at the bottom of the swirled grey paper
churns with a hundred soaked wings,
stumbling down into the air
consumed with choking murder in mind
and mindlessness. Your daughter
wide-eyed watches from the window—
as the nest drools mortal illness
from the garage eve closest to her pink swing set.
Protect her, that's the main ingredient
driving your finger on the
chemical-release button. You think
yourself some kind of hero, but
she's crying streaks as hornet after fuming hornet
flings itself out into the sunshine
against the colony's damning
and their death, yellow-black bodies
swirling, striking the pane and curling
on the window ledge, stingers throbbing
in mad attempt to repay dirty for dirty.
You think you've run far enough away,
you're relief-laughing, and she sees you.
She doesn't understand how such stings
destroy muscle, the pain and poison
they convey. You've spared her that lesson.
Job over. But she begins pounding
against the barrier, and you know
you are a mean silly man, someone
she does not like. She only sees bodies.

Who doesn't want to be a hero in a child's eyes? Who doesn't want to spare a child from pain? Who doesn't proceed with best intentions? But—who doesn't, in certain instances, come up short? I have tried, many times, to justify my actions: the killing of a spider to calm my wife, returning a hook-injured fish to water and telling myself that turtles will feed upon the ruination I've inflicted, smoke bombs down chipmunk holes compromising the backyard's leech field that would be expensive to fix. But if a child watches me in these instances, what exactly have I taught this young, impressionable mind? It's certainly more comfortable if I don't ask myself these questions. There's a good chance that the answers might not be what I want to hear.

The Editors on "Hornet's Nest"

Who hasn't wished to revert to immaturity—to see again, if only briefly, a child's world of light and magic? Scott T. Hutchison approaches such innocence from a different perspective in his poem, focusing on the idea that children are, at heart, egalitarians, unable to summon the utilitarian distinctions on which adults must regularly act. The speaker here is not the virtuous child but her compromised father, who kills a nestful of hornets in order to protect his daughter. What the father doesn't see—what the child instinctively understands—is that *daddy is causing all the pretty black and yellow bugs to hurt.* The child has been "spared" a "lesson" in pain, but the cost has been her previous understanding of her father as valiant protector. Such are the exigencies of parenthood, one might say. But tell that to the little girl who "only sees bodies." (*-Torri Frye*)

Doug Ramspeck

Curries

It is not down in any map; true places never are.

Herman Melville

She was late arriving. First it was spouses
we discussed, children, jobs. Then curries
to order: Panang, Khao soi, sour. And finally
that distant summer in Escanaba: wraith mice
scratching walls, moonlight like chalk on a front
porch, long grass we rarely mowed . . . and
one lost evening when a cataract of smoke
drifted without warning across the yard. It clung
in air, suspended, gathering the way a train glides
past you in a dream, silent yet with great force,
as though a thing might be separate from
its powers. Come morning we followed a stream
bed etched into the earth, the way years etch
themselves into a body. Followed it to the abandoned
barn and stables down the road. The earth,
when we arrived, was charred black. Open hulls
of barn were foundering on the shoals,
ribs exposed, as though a sea had retreated
and vanished. Then the meal was over
and we stood. Cars shouldered their way down
the narrow street. Above, an oatmeal sky
churned at its center the way years roll out
of themselves, capacious and illusory.

Julie L. Moore on "Curries"

"Curries" is not unlike Doug Ramspeck's other poetry: resonant and rich with
original, peculiar images sustained, rather than threatened, by a riptide that

disturbs the poem's universe. I met the poet once at a writing center conference, writing center directors that we are. We know a thing or two about our dual roles of assistance to those in need and subversiveness against systems that cause such need in the first place. So also in "Curries," Ramspeck charts a course toward need between a man and a woman and toward Escanaba, not a city in Latin America or Spain but in Michigan, a trek through memory lit by the moon but fraught with "wraith mice." The voice in the poem enters a simultaneously nebulous and particular territory—a dream but not a dream, loud with a vision of smoke, blackened by a fire not seen but certainly felt. The flames burn beneath the surface, perhaps like the man and the woman's past ardor, "separate from / its powers" yet likewise "capacious and illusory" above them.

Julie L. Moore

Molasses

After twisting open the lid on the jar of molasses,
I raise the glass, inhale the earthy aroma,
part bark, part root of everyone
who gave me breath.
                           Comes my great grandmother Elsie,
her round body and gray hair pinned neatly in place,
her red gingham dress and rhubarb pie,
her Lebkuchen cookies. Her heart
the only day it failed, hours before my parents
caught us jumping on our beds and sat us down.
The first darkness of my childhood
pouring thickly over me.
                           Comes my grandmother Irma,
her dyed-blond hair and lanky frame,
her lemon meringue pies,
job at Motown Records in Jersey,
slipping vinyl discs into sleeves.
Her back broken from osteoporosis,
her lungs smothered
in the black gum of night.
                           Comes my mother Doris,
the brunette curls, hazel eyes, and wide hips
she gave me, her left-handed pitcher's arm,
loud laughter, banana bread, and yes, those Christmas
cookies. The high blood pressure she fears
will, in some future year,
cast a long viscous shadow
over her words, still her limbs.

> They are all here
as I mix the syrup with flour and sugar,
nutmeg and cloves, as I roll and cut
and bake the deep brown dough.
And dusted white by day's end,
I seem to walk with them
through rooms imbued
with the heart's heady scent.

Julie L. Moore on "Molasses"

The scent of molasses returns me to my mother's kitchen when my sister and I learned how to make Lebkuchen cookies for Christmas. We would churn out those cookies by the dozens, gifting them to our neighbors, our father's colleagues at the pharmacy he directed, and our family members, in a time that seems bygone. Now, that kind of days-long work feels not only passé but also nearly insensitive: Colleagues, friends, and family members alike are watching their diets, trying to lower their carbohydrate counts or go gluten-free, and following advice on the morning news shows on "how to survive the holidays and not gain weight." Yet those cookies' ingredients contain my family's matriarchal legacy. Every bite of Lebkuchen carries equal parts of love and lament, lives fully lived yet hard fought through the exclusive economies known to most women: immigrants like my great-grandmother, Great Depression survivors like my grandmother, and Baby Boomers like my mother. And it is my daughter's favorite cookie: She, too, appreciates nutmeg's good humor, clove's strength, and molasses's feminist flavor.

The Editors on "Molasses"

I appreciate the fact that this poem, when read aloud, flows very much like molasses. Moore makes us feel as if we readers are slowly meandering through her memories as she pours the ingredients and makes these cookies. The details assigned to each of the poem's women are perhaps the heart of the piece—the grandmother working in a New Jersey record shop is quirkily specific, for example—yet they don't detract from the notion that these women could be part of *any* family: old ladies who bake warm cookies and live long lives. The intrusion of their deaths into an otherwise sweet poem (in more senses than one) nods to the mixture of happiness and loss that we all face. (-*Katie Dickau*)

Brian Swann

This

hermit thrush turns dusk to
    a quetzal's tail and dawn to scarlet skeins,

lilac, curlicues of chrome, his song
    flexible as air, bending notes like little

bars of steel beyond notation, making riffs
    of cloud-scurry that tie Plato's string in knots,

bell-notes burgeoning, sounds coming rich
    and thick in which nothing's lost, so fast

they seem simultaneous. But this "shy and
    hidden bird" is not above a yodel or high-who,

wanting me to hear, wanting me to listen as he leans
    over from the pine to my open window, before

vanishing into the woods he makes, into
    the music he is.

Ann Lauinger on "This"

Brian Swann's beautiful poem "This" goes ekphrasis one better. It isn't easy depicting a visual object in words, but how much harder to capture music, and inhuman music at that. The risk is great: that the poet's song will seem paltry beside the song it invokes. "This" succeeds because it offers much more than mimesis, though it accomplishes that brilliantly. The seamless sequence of run-on lines from the title word through the middle of line nine imitates the liquid melody of the thrush in a cascade of gorgeous images— none static, all in transformation—that ask us to see, feel, hear, and maybe even to taste ("rich / and thick") in imagination what we can't hear in the flesh. But the poem has more to say than this feat of synesthetic mimesis, because the hermit thrush means more than its beauty. "This[!]" the title announces to us. Sure, two words later the demonstrative has its noun, but not before the importance of "this-ness" is proclaimed, calling us to a universe of particular presences and particular present moments. The poem's last word, "is," is contained in its first; triumphantly, they bracket the whole poem's meaning-as-being in a phrase: "This is"! We should remember that this bird does not just dissolve into his song but "yodel[s]" his identity: "[H]igh-who" is not the generic *heigh-ho*; he wants, as much as any poet who signs name to poem, to be heard, to be known. By now, the reader will have realized that "This" is a sonnet, unrhymed and un-quatrained but exhibiting the classic turn in line nine, in this case from song to singer. The old romantic rift between self and world, being and doing is healed in Swann's lovely and emphatic double ending, "vanishing into the woods he makes, into / the music he is." Still, it's the music of being that has the last word.

Ann Lauinger

The Amaryllis

"Not guaranteed to bloom a second year"
Means "Don't complain." But see the ambiguity?
Not "Guaranteed *not* to bloom": that would be clear.
You would have tended to it just like me:
Watered it, sunned it, checked for pests and disease,
And brought it inside well before its leaves,
Long drooping spears, got nipped by autumn freeze.

The anniversary of its splendor came
And went. I watered faithfully, I fed,
Without a hope of blooms. The only claim
It had on me was memory—the red,
Wide-mouthed clangor of its bells last year,
And weather mean enough to make a friend
Of anything that chanced to be in here.

I grew to think of it as a great-aunt
Subsisting on sweetened tea in my spare room,
All but forgotten—no trouble, but someone you can't
Evict. In May, a bulge I dared not assume
Would bud shot up, parting its oval case.
Some grief relaxed its spiky jaws and fled,
Unlooked-for scarlet giving brilliant chase.

Ann Lauinger on "The Amaryllis"

For once, if anyone should ask, I can say truthfully, "This poem really
happened." I was given a gorgeous red amaryllis one winter, and, after the
blooms faded, I dutifully followed, through the subsequent seasons, as best I
could, the instructions on the little tag around my plant's neck. I knew full
well, however, that my best was far from what the horticulturist ordered. The

next winter happened to be very hard for me in more ways than the weather. A pessimist by nature, I was surprised and transported when the amaryllis bloomed again, feeling, against all reason, that I'd received a second gift, though I couldn't name the giver. The poem's rhyme scheme spontaneously started in the first few lines I sketched, and I decided to keep it. I usually find it easier to write about my feelings when I have some formal requirement to tend to; minding these rhymes seemed to—I'm not sure what—distract my inner censor? protect my vulnerable self? Both of these, probably; also, it was fun.

The Editors on "The Amaryllis"

Is "The Amaryllis" a metaphor for the writing of poetry? A crazy idea, you say, but note that the poem's speaker is drawn to work that is both repetitive and almost certainly futile. The plant, like the poem, must be "tended," yet it "guarantee[s]" nothing. Its "only claim" is "memory." It is "no trouble"—one can almost see the poet winking there—but neither can it be "evict[ed]."

Such are the leaps one prepares oneself to take when reading Ann Lauinger's coy, delicate poems—each one a "brilliant" flower; each one chasing away some "spiky-jaw[ed]" grief. We've been lucky enough to publish three of them over the past several years, and in each case they've lingered in my mind for weeks, blooming into newness as formal delights have given way to a deep appreciation of the poet's mastery of syntax. Lines eighteen and nineteen provide a master-class: "In May, a bulge I dared not assume / Would bud shot up." Twelve words, thirteen syllables, all perfectly arranged. Oh, and the poem rhymes. This is truly a composition that has been "watered" and "sunned." (*-Graham Hillard*)

Amy Fant

The Night Matthew Tried to End the Life of a Dying Deer

We awoke to waves in our chest—
that quickness of heart, pushed from a dream
at 2:00 am to darkness.
It was the doorbell. My father, half-robed,
his voice wrestling with wakefulness: *Stay there—*
don't come down, his opened palm keeping us on the stairs.
There you were, bloody hands and all,
fumbling with the front door. And you were crying.
I could only see a half of you: your sleeve
wet with crimson blood, your hand
wiping and wiping, your mouth was a line.
This is it, I thought.
You had finally done it, letting sadness
off the long leash. All those afternoons
we thought you gone, imagining you
in the car, in your room, in the woods:
your body pulsing until it wasn't. All that blood.
Your shoulder brushed the white wall.
I could only hear a half of you: *A deer—I tried.*
The road widens where you'd driven your truck into the deer.
Panicking with its life, you had pushed a knife into its chest
because you wanted death a little quicker.
Our dad, a shotgun, and you still red and breaking
all vanished back into the night.
When you returned, I watched you lock the bathroom door,
the water ran. I wondered: Did you sink onto
the bath's edge to place your face in your hands,
a breath escaping, like prayer, through the slice of your lips?
Did that blood feel close enough to yours this time? Did it leave
you wanting? In the morning, the road was bathed
with red, a haunting.

I always reiterate to my introductory creative writing students that identifying with a piece does not mean that the piece is successful—that we must not respond based solely on our own experiences. Thus, at first, it felt hypocritical to write about this poem, or as if I would have nothing to say once I got past my initial reminiscences: that lonely, desperate drive through the Arkansas night, my head screaming louder than whatever was on the radio; the beautiful doe that shot into the glare of my headlights; the crunch of bone and metal. Of course, this memory is only a half of the story. The other half is in the shared language of demise and mercy, in the blood sacrifice that "want[s] death a little quicker." The title's use of the phrase "tried to end the life" suggests that euthanasia and suicide are related impulses, the same blood sacrifice. The other half of the story is also in the rhetoric of questions rather than relayed experiences—in asking rather than telling if two different faces of death form the same coin. Matthew likely couldn't tell you "if the blood [felt] close enough" to his; I couldn't, either. We never know what is enough, what sacrifice will transform darkness back into light. We are haunted by sacrifice's red stain.

Emily Allen

Words Borrowed from Sensible Things

That first duplex we shared, the neighbors' front walk
was always a pastel collage of backwards numbers
and letters, blurred by the tracks of a miniature fire truck
overturned in the drive. We wrote notes in stolen chalk
to our future children, as heat lightening spiderwebbed
the cloud banks between distant glass towers.
In pink, you printed: *There are places where the sky*
gets dark at night. Go there and name the stars.

I told you we had our own constellations:
subdivisions, sidewalks, a line of streetlights
with no darkness between. Nights you worked I'd walk
without destination, listening to the patterning of sound,
of need, of people squawking to themselves
like so many flockless birds. I needed to understand
the city's conversation with the earth, the way the subway
shook bedrock. When the baby came, we called him Polaris.

Idiopathic, they said of his silence, an unnamed expressive delay.
My mother reminded me my first word was lake,
then nothing else, for months, like winter migration.
Syllables would come: We must be patient like water.
He was pointing at everything with wheels,
growling and sputtering like an engine with low oil,
when suddenly you said, *car, car, he's saying car.*
All I could do was stutter.

This was how I came to know the interstate's
habits like a birdwatcher, its deliberateness, its rush.
Internal combustion, the timing of the tongue's
force against palate, different dialects: I have forgotten
my words, the river's current. I have forgotten the sky
for a knot of taillights mapping the northern horizon.
Polaris, I know only turbulence and order,
cacophony and silence. Learn from my losses.

Emily Allen on "Words Borrowed from Sensible Things"

"Words borrowed from sensible things" is a quote from Emerson's "Nature"
describing the origins of language. Writing this poem felt similarly organic and
was necessary not just as a poetic transition but as catharsis. It shaped itself to
fill a space between poems, then, no longer confined, expanded to shape a
manuscript. My life, my writing, had been hijacked by a grief I could neither
speak nor ignore, and my work had meandered accordingly; in the aftermath,
I was left with islands of starkly different experiences that now demanded
attention, navigation. As I walked my neighborhood after the Texas heat had
evaporated from the pavement, the freeway was white noise, and every family
out for an evening stroll reminded me of what I wasn't, what I had chosen
not to be. Meanwhile, my friend named her son Orion, and my eighteen-
month-old nephew's complete silence taunted us all. Stasis with the city I
called home—only because language proves upon the world—was reaching
back to astronomy, back to that star map of my rural childhood. The poems
needed to expand, wanted a baby.

Lauren Camp on "Words Borrowed from Sensible Things"

It is the sounds of this poem that first catch my attention. I trust a writer who
is willing to settle me in a place ("That first duplex we shared, the neighbors'
front walk"); I will follow the path she takes me on. Allen's use of hard
consonant sounds, first for material objects like "tracks" and "truck," leads
me to the harder and more intangible "turbulence," "stutter," and
"combustion." The poem constellates many relationships: between two
people, person to city, person to child, person to silence and order. Each

stanza is a chance to shift, to see something fresh: new images, new visions and meanings. The poem asks to be read again and again. The shape of the poem—four stanzas, eight lines each—makes it seem stable. But there is much here that unnerves that solidity, and nothing in the poem is as even, as reliable, as it would seem on first glance. There's such absence in the words themselves, a loss mapped onto everything that is discussed.

Lauren Camp

How Could I Not See

Morning bubbles up. I share a table
at a small café with my husband's father.
Left by spouses who've gone here and there,
we catalogue our silent details. Together,
we share only brief points of view.
He grips a novel and the round table
between us. The bread is white, juice pulped
and tangy. He eats contemplation heartily,
always stooped into it. I sip at tea.
All our words could fill a cup, but then
he asks if I know Dickinson's 465
("I heard a fly buzz—when I died—").
I nod, unsure. Light eases in the corner.
I watch his mouth, and only that, as he recites
and tastes the slight translucent phrases.
I note his mouth's small moisture,
and how the poem dwells in him
like yeast, how it rises in perfect order
until the salt of *Signed away*
What portions of me be / Assignable—
I begin to see the tangled space
of all his senses. *And then the Windows failed,*
he says with shuffled breath, and he is
nearest me, but blurring. The poem pursues us,
not yet finished. He is blinking.
I could not see to see—he nearly weeps.
There is no end to the dark mystery of the old.
At that moment, I ache to know if he's afraid
of dying, or of living in the endless room
of being dead, but we don't talk. His blue eyes
start thickening. He pours some coffee, stirs it,
and we sit awkward in ourselves again,
in the only available chairs, with two flat faces.

Lauren Camp on "How Could I Not See"

I began "How Could I Not See" in February 2011, one week after listening to my father-in-law recite, from memory, an Emily Dickinson poem he said he hadn't thought about in many decades. We had both taught workshops at the San Miguel Writers' Conference the day before. He's typically very quiet but becomes animated and sentimental about literature and films. It was my uncertainty about his moist eyes as he recited that made me want to work the experience into a poem. Later that day, I jotted down a few notes on his delivery, along with a mishmash of other memorable bits I'd heard at the conference. When I returned home, I typed up my notes and began sussing out a poem. Some of the language in the final version was there at the start, but the poem went through twelve revisions, growing longer and longer, then shorter, before I deemed it done.

Marjorie Stelmach on "How Could I Not See"

Lauren Camp opens with a perfect image: bubbles of morning light—brief, fragile—followed by a catalogue of details: a woman and her husband's father, a round table, bread and juice. We witness his hunger for contemplation, her small sips. They share only words enough to fill a cup. But *their* words aren't the point: He has a poem by heart.

"Light eases in the corner" as he begins his recitation, and now it's all about tiny shifts within both Dickinson's poem and Camp's: the dimming vision of the person on the deathbed, the blurred vision of the woman at the table. Dickinson's words are in charge now, in pursuit of these two whose habits of self have left them both poised to flee. But they stay—meeting in a "tangled space." And then it's over; they are "awkward in [them]selves" once more.

The speaker in Camp's poem makes no claim of understanding. "There is no end to the dark mystery of the old," she tells us. The two are back "in the only available chairs," returned to reticence, to solitude, because our "Windows" *will* "fail," as will poems if what we ask is understanding. If what we ask is to *see*, Camp for a moment makes it possible.

Marjorie Stelmach

Lullaby for Two Voices

> *I was born at a time when most young people had lost their belief in God for much the same reason that their elders had kept theirs—without knowing why.*
>
> Fernando Pessoa, *The Book of Disquiet*

My earliest recurrent fear—hooves,
riding down on me hard in the dark—
turned out to be my heart.

God loved me, back then;
framed above my bed, Jesus the shepherd
pastured his flock beside still waters—
but my room was as dark as wet black ink,
and all winter the hoof beats drew nearer.

Years later, in a sermon I've otherwise forgotten,
a preacher explained the psalm's *still waters*:
sheep, he claimed, have an innate fear
of swiftly moving streams.

As if, by this fact, he might nail truth to faith.
Or faith to the fearful workings of the earth.

My mother, deep in dementia now,
repeats the 23rd Psalm without a misstep.
I'm the one who winces as she nears
the valley of the shadow.

I want to think hers is a pure and fearless faith,
but there are days she grips my hand so hard
she shakes,

and I've nothing to offer her—nothing of truth,
nothing of death.

Sometimes we sing old hymns together.
Neither of us knows the words.

By their second spring, lambs are all but grown,
grazing meadow grass beside a race of snow-melt,

or ranging the slopes where repeatedly, stupidly,
they strand themselves out on some
perilous rock outcropping.

And there they stay,
hunkered at the brink, bleating:
error unto death, error unto death.

If I were their shepherd, they'd be taken
by the wolves. I'm terrible at rescue. Worse,
all I'd offer them is cynical advice:

*Wiser by far than the paths of righteousness
are the promptings of fear.*

These days, it's my own uneven history of vigilance
that wakes me to the dark, reaching for words
to talk my heart down from the edge
of abandonment.

Heart, I say, *don't fret;
there's nothing here to fear.*
But the hoof beats. And the plummet.
And the wolves.

Lately, though, I'm weary of the lies I tell myself.
Is this what it means to lose your faith?

Often now, my mother misplaces her words,
replacing them with smiles of apology
to break my heart.
To restore some kind of balance,
I bring too many words of my own
to the Center.

On my worst nights, I picture her lying in the dark,
listening to the pounding of her heart.

In my good dreams, we're singing—a slender song,
a lullaby. *There, there*, I sing. Meaning: *here, I'm here*.
Where we need fear no evil.

Hush, now, I sing. *Hush*, meaning this:
when our words have disappeared, the workings
of the earth will grow kinder.

Marjorie Stelmach on "Lullaby for Two Voices"

"Lullaby for Two Voices" is one in an ongoing series of poems I've been
working on for the past two years, each with an epigraph from Fernando
Pessoa's *The Keeper of Sheep* or *The Book of Disquiet*. I'm trying to inhabit the
voice of his poems, a voice that seems accustomed to a pace slower than my
own, more compassionate, more honest.

This poem is about the increasing uselessness of words as the demands of my
life change: about the thinning of those comforting words of childhood, the
false comfort of facts in a context of sorrow, my fear of the hard truths words
can tell if I truly listen, and my stubborn hope that, in the end, there will be
something more than words to ease her leaving. Maybe music? Maybe a kind
of faith I have yet to understand?

My mother is losing her words now. It frightens us both. I'm trying, as the
Alzheimer's progresses, to be equal to her changing needs, to learn how to be
a caregiver in a truer sense of caring and giving. Pessoa's meditative cadences
have helped. There's a fair distance to go.

We stitch lullabies together from images and melodies to ease the transition from one form of consciousness to another. Those who sing lullabies know they serve not only to relax the child listening but also the singer. When the mind is racing at the end of a hard day, a lullaby soothes and unites us.

This poem forms a lullaby with pictures and thoughts from across time and space, and its title emphasizes two voices. The mother calms the speaker, both when the speaker was a child and now, in her adulthood. The speaker tries to do likewise but struggles with the role reversal—no longer a child but always a child, and now a caregiver to a mother with dementia, a disease that terrifies with its unpredictable progression. Even while singing, the speaker worries she's losing her way.

The poet situates the poem's end not in fear, however, but in power. After exploring the parent/child dynamic, the poem transcends it to tap into a natural force hinted at throughout, beyond these two characters. In doing so, this lullaby reaches out to soothe us, even at this bewildering point of transition, at which neither speaker nor mother nor the reader knows what's next in coming.

Angie Macri

Green Snake

Asleep in the afternoon, such heat is unclear,
as if the winter's flame under the faucet
grew. That single spot lit to keep the pipes
from freezing when the power was out,
a candle waxed onto the drain, swells
and consumes everything.

The ceiling fan spins a burned flower
through air thick and still, like sluggish creeks.
It might build to afternoon clouds that coax
the sky to rain. On the living room floor
under spinning blades, I forget anything
but such a chance.

After sleep, I walk out, barefoot into
the yard's erratic cut of grass. I step
on the hose my mother uses to pull
water from the well to wash our clothes.
It slides away, across my arch. Green snake,
you'd better run.

You have a weedy skeleton, and my grandmother
has already shown she will hack all snakes apart
with the garden hoe. My father argued
she should leave them alone, but she grew up
in other days, of keeping a stick of wood
by the back door

to push the snakes away, of children seen
not heard, of rods not spared. Sometimes
we find shed snake skins. They have crawled out,
after a thoughtful spell, their new scales
so bright across their length, healing, surging
as if heaving heat.

I won't tell them you were here for a week
at least. For this, work for me new feet
of scales and an underside that measures
waves through earth, of fault lines, footsteps,
the whirring, sharpened blades that keep
all close.

Angie Macri on "Green Snake"

This poem originates in the one-of-a-kind sensation of a snake sliding across
the arch of my foot. Even though I was little at the time, as a child raised in
the church I thought immediately of the verse "he will crush your head, and
you will strike his heel." But I hadn't hurt the snake, and it hadn't tried to bite
me.

If you let it, a poem's structure can help reveal its meaning. The first stanza
set the pattern for the rest of this poem, and the two stanzas that followed
cemented that form. This poem uses six-line stanzas, with each last line falling
short.

Oftentimes when I'm writing, I meet myself coming around a corner. The
speaker of this poem occupies a place in the middle. She's trying to negotiate
different parts of her world, from ecological extremes to diametrically
opposed perspectives. How can she balance things so that everyone is happy?
There's no way to succeed in that position. She makes a bargain with the
snake that I didn't have the presence of mind to make. Or maybe I did. This
poem sets me free.

"Green Snake" echoes Claudia Emerson's fabulous "Natural History Exhibits," whose speaker confesses to having grown up "around / women who would kill any snake, never / mind what the men said . . . ." Here, Angie Macri sidesteps altogether that intractable debate (between "grandmother" and "father" in this case) and proceeds instead down a third path: She addresses the snake directly, asking it for "new feet / of scales and an underside that measures / waves through earth . . . ." An unusual request? Yes, but one that proceeds from the perfect logic of the poem.

This is, after all, a work in which the flame of a single candle "swells / and consumes everything"—in which the ceiling fan is a "burned flower," and the air is as "thick and still" as "sluggish creeks." Who but a snake, with its "weedy skeleton," could offer respite, revision, *escape*? Who else could coax from a child so furtive a promise?

In its early issues especially, a literary magazine must decide what it wants to be. Let the record show, then, that "Green Snake" was the first poem we ever accepted for publication. (-*Graham Hillard*)

Al Maginnes

What the River Built

The river might have offered escape
      had it not run too quickly to allow
entrance into the brown swell
      of its veins. Below what we could see
lay rocks fractured to angles and blades,
      the mud of its belly folding over
thousands of arrowheads too flawed
      for flight, so drowned instead.
Without trying, the river built
      one more obstacle that made
a fortress of the town. Ronnie Gayden,
      who had kin buried in almost
every graveyard in the county,
      claimed an uncle or step-grandfather
drowned diving from the rail trestle
      into the river not long after
the dam was built. Another text
      for nightmares, a water harsh
as the God we were taught to fear.
      Like all deities', the river's threat
was endless and still is
      for a boy eyeing the twists
and braids of current, figuring
      his weight against the water's spread.
I live close to lakes now, man-cut
      and deceptive islands of water.
In warm months, water takes back
      a few of us land-walkers,
releases them only when they are
      more water than earth, one means
of escape from that almost-nameless town.
      And we who lie burning with

the desire for other places find ways
        over ancestors drowned by time
or legend, their bones gone
        soft and milky in a universe
made finally of water.

Ava Leavell Haymon on "What the River Built"

An insular small town bounded by a dangerous river and a harsh God, the desire for and seeming impossibility of escaping alive, and more than one drowning: What more does a story need? This story, though, is not content with that. We know this for sure when we encounter the lines "Like all deities', the river's threat / was endless." As if the story wants to escape boundaries of its own, it narrates itself in the voice of a poem, with lines that shift indentation back and forth and begin to look like ripples in water, and with the singing sounds of lullaby vowels and few hard consonants. A poem-voice that invokes ancestors "drowned by time / or legend, their bones gone / soft and milky in a universe / made finally of water." A poem that warns all "us land-walkers" that this is our fate, too, whether or not we manage to escape for a while.

Ava Leavell Haymon

Aubade

Behind the cholla cactus, a smooth arc of sky
whitens for half an hour, a first cup of coffee.
Backlit honeybees work the fuchsia blooms.
Their baggy abdomens halo with neon fuzz.

The bees' tenor hum calls back
an early morning dream: my teacher's house
and two shape-shift sons. I answer
the older one's questions. The younger one
is crying. The teacher—always
so kind!—doesn't seem to hear.
I wander kitchen, bedroom.
I don't know where things are.

At once—piercing the screen of bees,
cactus branches, spines, florescent petals—
a diamond laser focuses at just my eye level.
The sun disk itself, easing over Virgin Mesa.

It outlines—how could I miss this?—
a hummingbird. My hands uncurl.
In the blazing silhouette, no quick nod
just below the tiny skull, no champagne-flute
tipping of the entire bird, but instead a hinge
between neck and body, surprising
as a new knuckle in my 50 year thumb.
A bow, like ox's neck lowered to yoke,
the likeness all out of pace and scale.

Sensei, I give you up.
You've walked with me here,
a child's imaginary playmate. I've waited
for years to show you the mountains—hoarded
the frost heave, tamarisk, a desert bluebird.
This is one detail too many.

I wanted to be your excellent guide, offering
earnest lists of wildflowers, conifers
walking the Rockies from the boreal forest
at the top of the world, the rift in continent
that in its inexorable violence
affords the Rio Grande a valley
it did not have to carve.

The dream rises again: I carry your younger son
on my hip. Why can't you see his loneliness?
Holding him, I find your study
and it is my father's, the same
yellow mattress on the floor, crowded in
with the bookcases and sermons.

My eyes cannot meet the growing sun.
I look down. My hands, the broken halves
of a bowl of light. Released,
the hummingbird bends its supple neck
toward the colorless center of another flower.

Ava Leavell Haymon on "Aubade"

"Aubade" has long been a favorite poem of mine. Although the glorious
experience of the hummingbird in dawn light in the New Mexico desert
"really happened," the backstory will not be clear to a reader. The backstory,
however, is not what the poem concerns itself with. *Sensei* refers to a teacher
very important to me. I never addressed this mentor as "Sensei," and in fact it
took more than a year before I settled on that word for the poem. The term is

an honorific in Japanese, I've been told, meaning something like maestro or spiritual master. None of this comes from the backstory, except that air of respect and a kind of unspoken mystery. Do we ever understand the deep hold an important teacher exerts upon us? Upon our timeless dream life? Is any human worthy of this trust? Can any human live up to this?

Bobby C. Rogers on "Aubade"

Every sunrise is a parting. The writers of aubades have always known this. In Ava Leavell Haymon's lovely poem, a dreamworld with its fluid meanings gives way to sunrise over a New Mexico mesa, its twilit hues at least as nuanced and changeful as the dream it is dissolving. Haymon inhabits this liminal world with a consummate moral attention anyone familiar with her work will immediately recognize. The dream is a mournful dance of lost teacher and father, no more interpretable and no less beautiful than the first-light gathering in the landscape. She calls her teacher *sensei*—the parts of the Japanese word mean "previous birth"—and knows that the borning day's beauty, like the mystery of dreams, is being sharpened by the finality with which it has already begun to leave us. The aubade is a tragic form.

Bobby C. Rogers

Rain Crow

> **rain•bird** (rān´bûrd´), *n.* any of several birds, esp.
> the black-billed cuckoo (*Coccyzus erythropthalmus*)
> and the yellow-billed cuckoo (*C. americanus*), that
> are said to call frequently before a rainstorm.
> [1910-15; RAIN + BIRD]
>
> > *Random House Dictionary of the*
> > *English Language*, 2nd Ed.,
> > Unabridged

Until I learned better, the song of a mourning dove could make me
    homesick. I might be walking to breakfast down Melrose
    Avenue
in Knoxville, my first weeks up at school, and a wind-slurred call
    would startle me homeward. I must have still believed
the town I'd forsaken was the only place that could produce a sad
    sound. Why shouldn't the rest of the world harbor a wild bird
    or two
with mournful songs to sing? That fall whenever the phone rang,
    some voice from home came on the line to describe the
    circumstances surrounding
the death of another high school classmate. A dangerous time,
    those first stridings into the world, not knowing what you'll
    need to fear or even the name

it went by. More than one suicide that fall. And then Kirby was
    killed driving home at 3:00 in the morning after playing bass
    guitar
in a nameless bar band. I had almost stopped thinking about it
    every single second when *The McKenzie Banner* arrived with its
    hometown news

and gossip. There above the fold on page one was a picture of a
   volunteer fireman pointing a hose at the burning car to cool
   it down
so he and his help might get at it with the hydraulic cutter, in no
   particular hurry. People who care more about these things will
   tell you
the rain crow is a species of cuckoo, secretive and rarely seen save
   in the heat before a storm hits, but where I come from

the rain crow was the mourning dove, its *coo-coo-coo* heard as
   plaintive whether it is or not. Outside of hunting season, one
   was perched
on every fencepost, flocks of them evenly spaced along sagging
   power lines. When the sky grew cloudy and made ready to
   rain the birds would take wing
to dart and converse with added urgency as the wind kicked up.
   Their fair weather singing had been so much practice: now
   they dared us to write
consolation onto the notes of their song. I could love the folk
   wisdom handed me even if I couldn't believe it was true. The
   world doesn't need a bird's singing
to make it any sadder, but what harm trying to match a few words
   to the dove's breathy triplets? The rain will come—if not just
   now, then soon enough.

Bobby C. Rogers on "Rain Crow"

To subscribe to *The McKenzie Banner* visit <u>*mckenziebanner.com*</u>.

Todd Davis on "Rain Crow"

Like so much poetry, "Rain Crow" looks backward, attempting to situate its
speaker in another time and place, to make sense of the past in the present-
tense act of writing. The poem's long lines take their own sweet time to cross
the page, leaving a rent in the fabric where the poet confesses to a bout of
homesickness that serves as the poem's impetus. He offers up a version of

himself: young man off to college in Knoxville, discovering that the world beyond the town he's forsaken harbors "a wild bird or two / with mournful songs to sing." News of the deaths of high school classmates that first reached him by phone is taken up in a refrain as the same stories are sung by his hometown newspaper, delivered to his college mailbox. And so a front-page photo transports him to the carnage of a friend's fatal accident, "volunteer fireman pointing a hose at the burning car to cool it down / so he and his help might get at it with the hydraulic cutter, in no particular hurry." Fitting for a poem that also seems to be in no particular hurry, allowing what must be spun to slide smoothly from the bobbin, its insight woven through misdirection. Bobby C. Rogers knows how to tell a good story, reminding me of my Kentucky grandfather come into town once every two weeks for supplies, making a day of it to play checkers, to squat on the courthouse lawn with other farmers. I hear his drawl as I read this poem, words lengthened to fit the tongue, the poet preaching that "The world doesn't need a bird's singing / to make it any sadder, but what harm trying to match a few words to the dove's breathy triplets?" And all there is to say about that is *Amen*.

Todd Davis

Visible Spectrum

> *. . . we both believe and disbelieve a thousand times an Hour,*
> *which keeps Believing nimble.*

> Emily Dickinson

June light drapes itself
across the hay shocks
Jacob Peachey gathered
with his sons
yesterday afternoon.

New grass already sprouts
at the base, and in a few days,
when the hay dries, he and his sons
will lay up the shocks in the loft.

I don't think Jacob knows
how Monet painted haystacks
obsessively, stepdaughter
wheeling canvases in a barrow
so he might work at refining
the aspect of light
as it slid down the roof.

This time of year the sun
appears a little before five
and lasts until nearly ten.
Jacob values the light
that illuminates the work
he and his sons must do.

Next week he'll send
his milking cows
into the field
to eat what fell
and was left behind,
as well as what's new
and just growing.

I wonder what the grass feels
as the cows bend to tongue
each blade, releasing the light
that's been stored
through April and May.
Jacob faithfully studies
the light, notes
with nimble believing
the way it ripples
over everything
it touches.

Some days, after mucking
the stalls, like Monet
Jacob counts the layers
of light, marveling
at the fragility, his hand
passing through the visible
spectrum, as the sun
slips into the gaps
and shines brightly
between the barn's
rough boards.

Todd Davis on "Visible Spectrum"

I've lived most of my life in rural regions where Amish families farm, and I'm
grateful for their presence, for the example of living a life centered upon
community and a peaceful faith. At the same time, because of my love of the

arts, I've often wondered what might be missing from the lives of some of my Amish neighbors whose encounters with painters like Claude Monet is limited at best. On a June day, when I saw Jacob Peachey and his sons gathering hay into shocks to dry, I thought of Monet's paintings of haystacks, the artfulness of the light those paintings reveal. I began to compare Monet's deep, nearly obsessive attention to hay as an artistic medium with Jacob's equally absorbed attention to hay as a practical matter of living on his farm. One of my favorite writers, David Kline, is an Amishman from Holmes County, Ohio. David has published several books, including *Scratching the Woodchuck*, that pay homage to often overlooked moments in nature. In cutting the hay, in binding it into shocks, in living intentionally with the land, it became clear that Jacob and his sons might have experienced a portion of what Monet experienced more than one hundred years before: the different angles of light; what that light reveals; even the possibility that such moments illuminate the way the sacred moves artfully among us.

Carolyn Oliver on "Visible Spectrum"

In this poem, Todd Davis makes ordinary light newly visible, extraordinary in both its scope and simplicity.

First we see the warm sunlight as it "drapes itself / across the hay shocks"—already I think of drapes as curtains, opened and closed to regulate the flow of light—and the languid connotations of "drape" is countered by the gathered hay, the work of physical labor.

Then we have Monet capturing light with paint—and I love the seamless way agricultural and artistic labor are linked: Jacob Peachey and his sons gathering hay; Monet's daughter hauling canvases in a wheelbarrow, which many of us would associate with gardens and farming.

While Monet values the light as light, it seems Jacob values the long summer light merely for its usefulness. But then comes the turn: the cows headed out to the pasture, to lap up the hay and the grass, making the stored light their sustenance. The poet turns back to Jacob Peachey, who, like an artist, "faithfully studies / the light" with Dickinson's "nimble believing," finding in it illumination and utility, energy and beauty.

Carolyn Oliver

Pneumonia

We woke to find a collar,
bubbled murk of mushrooms,
cinching the dying oak.
An unexpected kingdom
only our small son might enter.

Did he, unnoticed, step
through that fairy ring to graze
the pale lichen bursting
over the bark, or encircle
a low branch with his weight?

That night, the cough broke
free of his chest. His lips blued.

In a thin-lit cold room
his mottled arms embraced
the machine as if to root
them both to Earth. Waiting
behind the wall we saw white
bloom inside his fragile form:
plump cells hoarding water.

In our oak's sapling days
we would have feared the gasp
in the dark, his departure
to another realm, the "we" of our
lives shrunken, maybe silenced.

Many oaks ago, our mothers
whispered charms against the snare
pulling taut to steal breath.
Now magic is cloying pink,
and no magic at all—
merely swift deliverance.

Moon obscured, a threshing storm
ushers in a downy sunrise haze,
and laughter foams upstairs.
Outside, the old oak stands undressed
of leaves and fungal ruff; snapped
like a twig from a broken nest,
one damp stem points at our door.

We do not stop to count the ways
we too might have vanished
before morning, but wreathe ourselves
in gratitude, witnesses
to a phantom season cut short
before our own.

Carolyn Oliver on "Pneumonia"

It was October, our first fall in our first house, when our son came down with
pneumonia. It seemed to happen overnight, just like the appearance of a ring
of mushrooms in the front yard, though decidedly more frightening than
magical. I didn't link the two events until weeks after the illness had passed,
but once I learned about fairy rings, my mind leapt to changelings, left in
place of children spirited away by fairies, and that's where the poem started.

Remembering how powerless and afraid I felt in that X-ray room led me to
think about parents—some of whom no doubt believed in, maybe took
comfort in, the myths of fairies and changelings—keeping watch over their
sick children hundreds of years ago, when science and magic kept closer

company than they do nowadays. When that amoxicillin—the same bubblegum pink I remembered from my childhood—kicked in and our son's breathing eased, it felt like he'd been pulled back into our realm, like we'd been passed over, liked we'd escaped this time. It felt like magic.

The Editors on "Pneumonia"

Carolyn Oliver's "Pneumonia" speaks softly of the hushed lethality of nature as the speaker's son nearly slips from her grasp; it is a narrative of what *would* have been a sudden loss at nature's swift hand. Intriguingly, the poem reads as fantasy, ethereal in nature. The world Oliver creates is one that makes no attempt to deny the magical or otherworldly: The narrator describes the disease as "another realm" and "an unexpected kingdom" that only her son can enter. Nevertheless, the poem is interwoven with very real maternal sentiment, as the "'we' of our / lives" threatens to become "shrunken, maybe silenced." The poem's power lies in part in its portrayal of so common a human experience: We have all had our "we" silenced or, at the very least, have experienced that possibility. Granted the occasional reprieve, we, too, can only "wreathe ourselves / in gratitude" every day that we (and "we") are still alive. (-*Christian Mack*)

Gail Thomas

Ambition

She tried to fly when she fell in love
        with Mary Martin as Peter Pan,
visible harness and all. Jumped off rocks,
        then trees. Only one broken
bone to show for suspended disbelief.
        Dreamed of wings sprouting
from shoulder blades, toes webbing like
        the swan brothers in Anderson's tale.
She would be one of them, willed herself not
        to bleed, to stop breasts from budding,
hips from curving. Not the sister on shore,
        sewing nettle coats with bloody
fingers. She would not be sentenced to earth
        with one wing.

The Editors on "Ambition"

"Ambition" looks at childhood darkly, disguising its perspective only by its
whimsical tone. The poem begins with a girl's love of Peter Pan and her
subsequent desire to fly, an impossible feat. Her determination is nearly
obsessive—she "[j]ump[s] off rocks, / then trees," leaving herself,
miraculously, "[o]nly one broken / bone to show for [her] suspended
disbelief." When her fixation accompanies her into adolescence, it meets yet
another impossible challenge as our heroine must now "will herself not / to
bleed." Accompanying all of this is a compelling rawness. The girl's dreams of
the impossible are inseparable from those of other children, and Gail Thomas
is not content merely to render them. Instead, she goes further, giving the
reader the sense that what is at stake here is the loss of innocence itself. The
girl's struggle against the laws of nature exist not only for the sake of
adventure but because she (perhaps rightly) fears the future. (-*Katie Riddle*)

David Shattuck

An Invisible City

I am at once the snow and the city hidden
underneath. Lunatics wrote these streets.

Tonight, even the moon shudders with the cold—
opening and closing, opening and closing.

When I sleep the dark-blind moth of your voice
flutters against attic windows.

I'm perfect at breaking apart
what my dreams so brutally perfect.

We light the bedside lamp at dawn
and watch the mountain step out of darkness.

April Ossmann on "An Invisible City"

Shattuck achieves a wonderful tension between beauty and potential harm, between dark knowledge and mystery, between agency and helplessness. The speaker is "the snow and the city hidden / underneath," which speaks to beauty, mystery, and multiplicity in the world and in the speaker, yet it is also true that "Lunatics wrote these streets," which suggests possible disquiet in the world and self, as well as the self-deprecating humor of the poet. It suggests also the impossibility of knowing *any* self when we have such hidden cities in us, when our voices are "dark-blind moth[s]." The speaker has agency that manages to feel somewhat helpless against lunacy and self-harm, as he's "perfect at breaking apart / what [his] dreams so brutally perfect." His fuller agency can be seen in the final couplet, yet even here it exists in part, because of the assistance of the partner/lover: Together, they "light the bedside lamp at dawn, / and watch the mountain step out of darkness." Note, however, that the mountain has agency, as well, and its stepping out of darkness could be either threatening or enlightening. A perfect tightrope of a poem!

April Ossmann

Sieve

Young men seem all edges
    and hard angles, shoulders
        like shelves, bellies like slides

to the most obvious
    of pleasures, young women
        all crisp curves, so round

and firm, their union seems
    geometrically insoluble.
        We soften as we age,

our geometries slipping
    and sliding, in small
        or quantum leaps,

bodies and definitions blurring
    as we morph, like mercury,
        into each new self we shape.

Living softens us
    to fill death's vessel,
        not like the solid we seem,

but the liquid we are—
    so we may slip the cup
        like the sieve it is.

April Ossmann on "Sieve"

I wrote "Sieve" sitting in my car in a parking lot, waiting to meet a friend and watching the passersby. Youth, aging, and mortality were much in my mind at the time, as I had lost two close family members in two years: my stepfather and father, both to cancer. Though poets, including myself, often write about mortality, such losses tend to bring the reality home to roost. I found myself wondering, with more than poetic urgency, how to live peacefully and contentedly with, or despite, the fact of my own mortality, as well as the loss of my loved ones. Even if I could have set aside such losses, I could not have avoided thinking about the changes in my middle-aged body. I formatted "Sieve" in what the poet Lynda Hull used to call terraced tercets, for the visual effect of each line undercutting the next, creating an airy and precarious foundation, like upside-down stairs or a sieve. The ending reflects my optimism and sense of adventure. We cannot know in advance what mortality will be like, so why not imagine a great escape, something lovely?

Shara McCallum on "Sieve"

There are many things that attract me to this poem. I'll start with its highly textured sonic field. Ossmann's diction seems guided by the ear as much as the mind. Words "slip" and "slide" from phrase to phrase, line to line, dictated often by alliteration's echo, in particular the "s" sounds that pervade. On the page, the indentation of each line of the tercets creates a similar cascading effect for the eye—a movement not unlike the filtering action of a "sieve" in the material world. An analogous process occurs on the level of sense, image, and idea, so that each turn in the poem feels inextricable from its form. The poem opens with depictions of men and women, suggesting that desire when we are younger is rooted in the angularity of the body, its perfect "insolubility." But this perspective quickly gives way to the poet's position on aging, that it "softens" the body and renders us "the liquid we are," preparing us for "death's vessel." As with its sound and lineation, the poem's logical progression embodies thought being strained—fast and falling, leaving the essential matter of living to be examined.

Shara McCallum

Ode to the Apple

I won't linger over your fall from grace,
your myth tainted by the facts.
If anything, it was a pomegranate,

not you, hanging in that garden. Instead,
I'll extol the virtue of your latest hoodwink act:
spliced and grafted, you replicate hunger

perfected. No surprise,
when I bite your flesh I detect
the perfumed rose, another we've lassoed

to desire. No surprise, fearing our own
rotting we wax your skin—its sheen
rivaling this dying star we orbit.

Maybe my father was merciful when
he peeled and sliced you open,
rendering you more palatable on a plate.

Oh, but that was some time ago,
and I've since grown a taste for tart, for bitter
lacing every sweet. And you

could never deliver the kind of freedom
I've long been after—to have no need
to make an Eden of this world, or any other.

Shara McCallum on "Ode to the Apple"

This poem comes out of my interest in form and is in some measure an
homage to two odes I adore: John Keats's "Ode to a Nightingale" and Yusef

Komunyakaa's "Ode to the Maggot." I've said this before elsewhere but will say it again here: My workings as a poet inside of traditional and invented poetic structures are guided by my belief that forms contain within themselves the shadow of their opposite. If the ode is the container we create or employ to extol the virtues of a creature or a thing, the form also has to hold (or hold at bay) the elegy. In both Keats's and Komunyakaa's odes, the poets' virtuosic admiration for the nightingale and the maggot, respectively, can only be perceived in relation to disease, decay, and mortality. Consider the last lines of each: "Fled is that music—do I wake or sleep?" (Keats); "Master of earth, no one gets to heaven / Without going through you first" (Komunyakaa). Using the ode, a form ostensibly meant to affirm the life of these noble or ignoble-made-noble creatures, the poets yet must reckon with death and grief interposing.

Grant Clauser on "Ode to the Apple"

I've always been attracted to odes, especially ones celebrating the small, mundane things we take for granted. The ode approach automatically opens doors, and McCallum's is a great example: how it honors the apple by offering a surrogate, the pomegranate, in its place in the Eden story. The multiple turns in this poem take you to amazing places, as when the abstract—"fearing our own / rotting we wax your skin"—gives way to the personal—"[m]aybe my father was merciful"—before coming around at the end to the Eden story once more. I admire the subtle soundplay of the poem, the sonic resonances of words like "fall" and "facts," "rose" and "lassoed," "rotting" and "rivaling." Those trails carry the reader from line to line, stanza to stanza, allowing for new discoveries when the poem is re-read.

Grant Clauser

Things She Couldn't Let Go Of

After she lost her leg
in a factory accident
when she was seventeen
my grandmother complained
for seventy-one years of cold feet
in the winter, phantom itches
when August brought mosquitoes
through the broken backdoor.
In her victory garden
she fought the perpetual
weeds that couldn't be stopped
but by digging out the root
like the chickens that kept kicking
after she cut off their heads
until she scooped out the guts.
When we emptied her house
we found a closet filled
with left shoes never worn,
each one stuffed with newspaper
to keep their shape.
The bed she'd shared
with Grandfather leaned
to one side, his body'd
spooned out a hollow
she'd avoided for years.
On every table, counter,
and drawer, graying photos
saved from before the war,
her long body in long dresses
leaning against black cars
or sitting on front porches,
small feet in pretty shoes.

Under the bed, tied in twine,
letters from a private no one knew,
the last few never opened.

Grant Clauser on "Things She Couldn't Let Go Of"

Like a lot of my poems, this one is a mix of family lore and fabrication—in this case, I lean more on fabrication. My mother's grandmother really did lose her leg, though I had my own grandmother in mind for most of the poem, because I knew her and could picture her (with two legs) in my head. My grandparents' house fascinated and sometimes frightened me; it was old and full of hidden things, hidden stories, and there I got in the habit of making stories up. The bits about the letters and the bed are also fabricated, but the chicken chopping was real, at least according to my father. In this poem, I mostly let the story create itself based on selections the language made. For example, the word *drawer* insisted that somewhere later I use the word *war*, and that's how the poem unfolded for me.

The Editors on "Things She Couldn't Let Go Of"

Though there is much that is worthy of praise in Clauser's poem, one of the things that continues to impress is how Clauser manages to make the idea of loss appear fresh and personal for the character of the grandmother. Disguised beneath "phantom itches" of a foot lost long ago is a deeper mourning that exists, for that character, as pictures of "her long body in long dresses / leaning against black cars / or sitting on front porches, / small feet in pretty shoes." These photographs remind the grandmother of what she has *really* lost. Through Clauser's masterful writing, the reader senses the grandmother's desire for who she once was; in the loss of her foot, she has lost part of herself, and time has done the rest. It is intriguing to see how Clauser extends this loss into the relationships that the grandmother was a part of, trading the soldier she once loved for a man defined here primarily by absence. This kind of writing demands empathy, and Clauser delivers it as he communicates complex emotions through mere possessions, snaps-shots of a bygone time. (-*Amanda Johnson*)

Renee Emerson

Tabernacle

The sheets are thin and white as a bill
we can't pay. Light and faces filter
through pink plaid, blue stripe. I am the parent
who builds the best tents. Ties sheet-corners
to the spindle-spines of kitchen chairs—
Mawmaw's chicken house walnut chairs,
the black-painted Walmart chairs from college,
the roadside abandoned chairs, all clustered
like a last supper.

In the living room, our only space for such
extravagances, they play sentinels to the lair.
I weigh down what is uncertain, leave a measure
of concealment, of places to view the outside.
Inevitably, the children find the most joy
in the careful structure collapsing.

The Editors on "Tabernacle"

In "Tabernacle," Renee Emerson rhymes "walnut" with "Walmart." It may
be that no further commentary is necessary.

How to resist, though, the poem's myriad charms? Very nearly a Petrarchan
sonnet, "Tabernacle" borrows that form's call-and-answer, embedding in the
"octave's" motley furnishings the economic realities that will make the sestet's
"extravagances" so heartbreaking. What, exactly, is the speaker "conceal[ing]"
from her children? What can their "joy" mean to her in the face of so much
"uncertain[ty]"? The poem doesn't quite answer, yet its very title manages to
suggest both refuge and impermanence—to suggest childhood, in other
words. The tabernacle, the reader will recall, was portable, transient. Yet the
Israelites met God there.

And what of that sheet, "thin and white as a bill / we can't pay"? If there is a better, more evocative simile anywhere in our archives, I can't find it. (-*Graham Hillard*)

Karissa Knox Sorrell

Salvation

When my daughter and I were drowning,
there was no choice of saving her or me;

there was only surviving.
Her eight year old arm

frantic, grabbing my shoulder,
my body disappearing beneath

the world of breath.
Everyone around us was

enjoying the summer sun
as the cool creek water

pulled us toward its netherworld.
I could not call for help

as my mouth was silenced
with the language of wet things,

drowned stones and skeletons
tucked along the riverbed.

At last, my husband saw us
and swam to her, pulling

her struggling body to safety.
For a moment I thought

I would slip into that underworld,
surrender my breath to the world above,

live among the buried remnants
where earth is current and song.

But finally I startled and swam
to the rocks, which I knelt upon,

my body heaving as if I'd just
left a great burden upon an altar.

Karissa Knox Sorrell on "Salvation"

This poem grew out of a real experience I had with my daughter one summer
at Fall Creek Falls in Tennessee. It was quite traumatic, and I felt the need to
release the event from my memory by writing it out. I chose short couplets to
mimic the movement of rising and sinking in the water; the white space
represents my silence as my head sank beneath the surface. As the poem took
shape, I realized how much it resonated with the idea of salvation in the
Christian faith, an idea that I was personally struggling with at the time. I felt
like I was floundering spiritually, facing the world that I'd always been told
was evil and seeing the good in it. I was able to use the setting of a swimming
hole to reflect my spiritual disorientation, caught between the place I'd always
known and the lyrical pull of a different world.

Angie Crea O'Neal on "Salvation"

How much space separates life from death, breath from song? Karissa Knox
Sorrell explores these questions in "Salvation," a poem haunted by what
could have been. Sorrell's story of a harrowing near-drowning experience
with her young daughter—a mother's very worst day—is rendered with such
precision. It deftly pursues an emotional undertow that pulls on the heart and
mind of the reader, as when Sorrell confesses, "For a moment I thought / I
would slip into that underworld, / surrender my breath to the world above, /
live among the buried remnants / where earth is current and song." Sorrell
brings us underwater with her, into its "language of wet things" with
"drowned stones and skeletons / tucked along the riverbed." We feel the
same weight on our shoulders, share in the burden of the sacrifice, plumbing

the depths of our own subconscious. How much space separates a mother from her daughter, self from other, I wonder after reading the poem? Perhaps it leaves us with questions that speak beyond the borders of motherhood and into our troubled world: How much space is really between all of us? How much of ourselves do we save when we give all to those we love?

Angie Crea O'Neal

Ezekiel

College Park, Georgia

Climb the streets of your first town, the one that still lives in the
rill of time, there in the melting blue before rivers. Go back and
make snow angels in the shallow dusting of thought, swing on the
branches of unknowing. Revisit and eat the scrolls that tell the story
of your youth. Search for old friends hanging on memory like
gossamer, tell them what you've learned, confess to them your faults.

Whisper all you've lost and retreat to those early places to feel the
weight of the sturdy wood beneath, wrapped tight in a soft lawn of
cotton blanket. Recall the hours scrubbing dirt from your fingers,
splinters coaxed from skin with tweezers. Don't forget about the pine
straw pillows, no fear of ditchwater, those close encounters under a
broken porch light. Walk roads with names you no longer remember

and wander along dirt paths that lead to forest dells, drop sticks in the
creek and watch them float east, towards the center. Retrace your steps
and find rest under a thick quilt of forgetting like a strong arm nestled
in the arch of your back. Climb the streets of your childhood, the place
that still holds you, haunts you like a dream, like a close, constant hand
on your shoulder.

Angie Crea O'Neal on "Ezekiel"

I grew up in College Park, Georgia, a town just south of Atlanta. In my most
creative and imaginative moments, my mind wanders, in some primal,
Wordsworthian way, back to the places there, all the old haunts—the dank
basement that we transformed into a hideout, the streets named after British
towns and landmarks: E. Hampton Court, Cambridge Avenue, Leicester
Lane. We lived on Cambridge, which ran parallel to Rugby. An anglophile
haven in the Deep South. Days before I wrote "Ezekiel," my mom and I,

feeling nostalgic, drove to the old neighborhood for fun. The line "Climb the streets of your first town" came to me driving around that day. Toni Morrison once said that writers are like water, always trying to find the way "back to our original place." I think that's what this poem is about—the strange, prophetic quality of our memories, the way the past shadows our present and illumes the future.

Karissa Knox Sorrell on "Ezekiel"

The first thing I noticed about this poem was the imperative, second-person form, which immediately allowed me to be present in it. I was deftly pulled into my own memories of childhood. The juxtaposition of proximity to, and distance from, one's past is the crux of the poem. Its innocent images of snow angels and pine straw pillows contrast with the language of aging and forgetting. We are always moving away from our childhoods, and yet they never fully leave us. Like the prophet Ezekiel, who was exiled from his home and trapped in Babylon, perhaps we become so caught in our adult lives that we forget to look backwards. The crisp, earthy images of this poem allow one's past to be concrete and imminent, so close you can taste it. One of my favorite lines in the poem is "Revisit and eat the scrolls that tell the story / of your youth." The poem compels us to feel the heft of our memories instead of exiling them, to allow the past to enter our fingers, our sight, our hearing, our bones, our cells.

Joanne Diaz

Erasure

The news of the death
                         broke down the barriers   of endurance.
            I lacked the
patience   to represent   that degree of grief:
                                         wretched mother
                                         at last transformed into a rock.

            The impact,
                         the hot alarm   of the soul—
my senses
                         subtle fire,
                         my ears,
                                         both eyes
the body weighed down
   by the surprise—

                 such an excess
                                 of human frailty.

[Note: This is an erasure of Michel de Montaigne's essay "Of Sadness."]

Austin Segrest on "Erasure"

What's happened is a cosmic erasure, and the poet responds in kind. Erasing a text about the ineffability of extreme grief, Diaz's elegy, a kind of unuttered utterance, also performs the text's claim. The confines of Montaigne's truth, then, become as inescapable as the confines of existence itself.

What's the difference between a cento and an erasure? Does it come down to process and position? Is the poet thinking more about what she "rubs smooth" (as in the Greek of "palimpsest") or about the words she preserves?

Is it anything like the difference between drawing and etching—where the plate's etched lines, taking no ink, are what *doesn't* show? Might the added limitation of erased-around word position function as a further productive constraint for the poet?

The late, great American poet Thomas Lux liked to say he was going to erase all the erasures everyone was writing. Yet this one stands out of the rubbed-away field. A unity of means and materials give this remarkable poem inevitability.

Austin Segrest

Errand into the Wilderness

1640

Fell into some trouble of mind
did the man from Weymouth.
In the night he cried out, "Art
thou come at last, Lord Jesus?"

With that, he sat up in his bed
did the man from Weymouth,
and breaking from his wife he leapt
out at high window

in his night shirt. A troubled fall
for the man from Weymouth,
a fallen man. "Enthusiast"
they'd call him. Through the snow

for seven miles he ran and prayed
did the man from Weymouth.
Knee-printed scenes of great distress
led them to the river,

traced into a boundlessness
the fallen man from Weymouth,
frozen stiff still kneeling where
he croaked his last "Lord Jesus."

Austin Segrest on "Errand into the Wilderness"

I wrote "Errand" while getting my Ph.D. at Missouri. I came across a
description of the incident in one of John Winthrop's letters from 1637. I see
I lifted several phrases directly: "A man of Weymouth . . . fell into some

trouble of mind." It's a delightful phrase, robustly 17ᵗʰ century. Yet it puts one in mind of Richard M. Jones's "Trouble in Mind": "Trouble in mind, I'm blue / But I won't be blue always . . . ." I like that dissonant echo.

"Fell into some trouble of mind," then, became the first line. The subject of the sentence plopped down into the next line: "did the man from Weymouth." Inverted thusly, it made for loose hymn or ballad meter; it also, as you can see, became a refrain. A second line refrain but no rhyme, you say?

I remember I had to work hard for "traced into a boundlessness": how to get from the snow-prints (yes, reported in the letter) to the last refrain and stanza. Edward Taylor!

> Lord, Can a Crumb of Dust the Earth outweigh,
>   Outmatch all mountains, nay the Chrystall Sky?
> Inbosom in't designs that shall Display
>   And trace into the Boundless Deity?

The title comes from Perry Miller's landmark Puritan study (1956).

The Editors on "Errand into the Wilderness"

"Errand into the Wilderness" transcends the poem's own land and steps into the delicate land of religious criticism. Austin Segrest uses beautiful language and clear images to sober those who deny the deadly potency of conviction.

The poem does not waste time getting to the point. Its opening lines—"Fell into some trouble of mind / did the man from Weymouth"—make clear that its subject has a problem. What is not clear, and what makes this poem so intriguing, is the lack of information regarding the man's "trouble." Was he misguided? Overcome by his "enthusias[m]"?

Segrest drops hints about the man's "fall" each of the four times he uses some variant on that word. Line seven's leap of faith is the poem's most important action, but perhaps its most interesting moment is the preceding metaphor: By "breaking from his wife," the man from Weymouth has become broken. Has a loss of reason done it, or has it been the overwhelming power of conviction? Whatever the case, the image is potent: a broken man exposed but faithful. (-*Katerine Avila-Pastor*)

Davis McCombs

eternal, restless

Wind cranks the handle on the grindstone made of ice,
hones one slim evening to a blade of light, then less;
then sparks go skittering among the trees. This is the way
it starts to snow, the way the trails he prowled in life are lit
by ice. The woman drifts to her window, clicks on a lamp.
Now maybe a gust, off-kilter, gathers up a body of flakes;
maybe it bristles, whimpers, but pretty soon it's scratching
at her door, and pretty soon she's dreaming of the past,
and maybe, just once, his name will cross her mind
like the shadow of an owl. Now even the night begins
to fidget, as if the pulse of rivers in his wrist were beating
to the throb of rivers underground, as if the owl were real,
as if it ever really snowed, or started to, like this.

Davis McCombs on "eternal, restless"

I wrote this poem several years ago now as part of a sequence of poems that
centers around the killing, on January 16, 1902, of the last gray wolf in the
area of Kentucky where I grew up. The event took place at a huge, cracked
bluff called Dismal Rock above the Nolin River, very near where my father
was born. Dismal Rock is also the title of my previous book of poetry and, in
fact, the wolf makes its first appearance in my work in a poem called "The
Last Wolf In Edmonson County," from that collection. I wrote the earlier
poem around 2005 or so, but I never could shake the feeling that I hadn't
finished with the story, that there was more to it, more to be said on the
subject. In a sense, it haunted me, even though in that first attempt at writing
about the wolf, I'd claimed not to feel haunted! Returning to the wolf
narrative led me to folklore, which then became the source for so many of the
poems in my latest book. I'm always happy when that happens: one poem
opening a door that leads to others.

First, the grindstone; then: the ice, the snow. Thus the poem moves from an imaginative space to the target of the metaphor, *the real* as a winter landscape. Thereby oriented, if only briefly, the land bears the memory of the departed. First a "he" and then that "he" as an imaginative space, the inner life of a "she." And thus the emergence of *her* as the poem's center of consciousness, haunted by an evocation of grinding, sharpening, snowing. First pain (the grind), then erasure (the snow)—erasure as both the occasion and the negotiation of pain, erasure as the context of loss and denial in which memory connects to figures in a landscape. What lies below is thus the mind within her mind; the evocation of rivers and blood, a wrist no less; the vague elements of tragic narrative that invisibly haunt the numbing silence of the snow. Thus the occasion for the poet's deft and surprising turn at the poem's end, wherein grief, partially recovered, partially repressed, renders all unreal.

Bruce Bond

Song

Some days the song of the small enclosure
takes you a little farther, deeper, less
by way of what it says, than how it shudders,
how it lends a body to the chaos,
a mirror to the air, blood to the hands
we lace in thought, as if to reconcile
a grief with what we cannot understand.
Some days a whisper shakes the heart's cathedral.
Not because our prayer is large. More
because it feeds a silence that is larger.
Come closer, say the atoms of the echoes.
Be small. Pull a chair to the fire,
to the pulse's will to proceed, to listen,
to close our eyes and tear the darkness open.

Bruce Bond on "Song"

This poem figures in the final section of my book of sonnets *Black Anthem*,
where I reflect on the power of music and its relation to the book as a whole.
Why write a book of sonnets, after all? Is it merely showy or acquiescent? Is it
politically or psychologically fraught, as a dominant, contemporary reading of
form—this form in particular—suggests? It is precisely because of the naively
rigid codification of form that I wanted to move the sonnet, the "little song,"
into a space more explicitly invested in otherness, including the otherness of
form and music itself. Music, however coded, is larger than mere code.
Likewise, it is smaller. The sense of enclosure need not exclude the spirit of
openness. After all, psychic integration (yet another sister of lyric musicality)
makes one a better listener. The body of the song can be imaginatively ours, if
only to take us out of ourselves, our codes, our pride, our preconceptions: to
pull us to some fire and let the chaos in.

In Donne, love "makes one little room an everywhere," but Bruce Bond's equally metaphysical, slant-rhymed sonnet, "Song," imagines a more isolated, solitary diminution. This "song of the small enclosure" takes its own advice, eventually shrinking its pentameter line to a tetrameter in its most urgent imperative: "Be small. Pull a chair to the fire." So where lies love in Bond's poem? The "heart's cathedral" would eagerly fill with devotion, sacred or profane, yet it's so fragile that "a whisper shakes" it. "Our prayer" tumbles into a far larger "silence" that is really no silence. Rather, its "atoms" vibrate with "echoes" instructing us: "Come closer . . . . Be small." Our prayer echoes back to us, clothed in atoms of air, like Donne's angels. Those rebounding echoes direct us forward, "to the fire"—domestic warmth—and "to the pulse's will to proceed" in a living world. We must "close our eyes" and, in doing so, deny emptiness, imagine meaning, and "tear the darkness open." Will light burst forth? With eyes closed, we can't tell. Finally, we are thrown back on imagination, on what the mind sees with inner vision, on the echoes in our ears—on "Song."

Jay Rogoff

Eating People Is Wrong

Each student writes a firmly fixed belief
upon the board. After their squibs on God,
abortion, and world peace, a skittery laugh
bubbles up at this dogma I have scrawled.

"Why do we call it wrong?" I ask. "Mere logic
can't make it evil; to say *a priori*
that cooking conscious beings is barbaric—
that's sentimental, narrow, arbitrary."

The students chew that over. So do I.
They're thinking of that monster epicure
Hannibal Lecter, fussing over Château
Haut Brion to complement human liver.

Montaigne reminds us anthropophagi
(Columbus coined the label "cannibals")
are fully human, just as you and I.
Caliban sings, dances, and seeks grace.

Our meat is poetry. Was Jeffrey Dahmer
(madman, pederast, and cannibal)
more wicked than, let's say, the Unabomber,
killing on ecologic principle?

The mind sees a hand or foot upon a fork,
or parceled people-portions for Idi
Amin. The new white meat, leaner than pork!
Among the Hua of Papua New Guinea,

all children must ingest their family's essence
to grow up fully human, so they're fed
sweat, urine, feces, blood—every excrescence,
plus flesh of friends and loved ones lately dead.

Chinua Achebe loved to tell this joke:
a cannibal was asked if he enjoyed
his diet. "Oh, yes, I love eating folk.
I want to eat everybody in the world!"

Eyes squinting under multicultural
illumination, we grope to consensus:
our class determines on a cannibal
lifestyle, if civilization so demands us.

The Donner Party, the Andes crash survivors—
my students sigh; some tears. More food for thought
while gathering their books, the class now over,
to head for lunch at commons (mystery meat).

Jay Rogoff on "Eating People Is Wrong"

At Skidmore College, we used to welcome new students with a gigantic, team-taught, interdisciplinary course called The Human Experience. In one course reading, "The Fixation of Belief," the American pragmatist Charles Sanders Peirce describes the process by which we come to believe what we believe. In my discussion sections, all students would write on the board something they believed strongly. Their beliefs ranged from factually demonstrable ("The earth revolves around the sun") to unprovable but firmly inculcated ("I believe in a caring God") to capricious but tenaciously held ("The Mets will win the World Series"). I liked to add "Eating people is wrong" because it focused discussion on how often we base beliefs and taboos on received authority rather than reasoning or scientific method. As for Chinua Achebe's joke, I heard him tell it after someone asked, "Whom do you want to read your books?" The tension between my poem's full and slant rhymes adds, I hope, to its comic queasiness, with the rhyme "Jeffrey Dahmer / Unabomber" a gift from the muse of silliness. Come to think of it, "a priori / arbitrary" isn't bad, either.

The Editors on "Eating People Is Wrong"

Jay Rogoff's poem is both humorous and startling: To read it is to wonder what, exactly, *this is*. One finishes the poem with—let us admit the point—a number of questions. A professor is talking to his students, but is the conversation at all believable? Can the poem's lovingly detailed invocation of cannibalism—"children . . . ingest[ing] . . . sweat, urine, feces, blood—every excrescence"—*really be happening?* I personally had to stop for a moment upon reaching the conclusion. What on Earth had I just encountered?! Yet it is the very weirdness of the poem—its silliness, its grotesque suspicions about the school cafeteria—that makes it so successful and fascinating. (*-Noula Arroyo*)

M. S. Rooney

Weavings

We are flesh and bones woven
from goods borrowed or stolen,
and we ask who and why
of tea leaves, of stars, of
a god we hear only in silences.

In the absence of answers,
we take up this pen, that music,
this lover, that thief, weave stories
that ravel or hold depending on
the slant of sun on blank pages.

We set lines to capture flashes,
those hints of knowing *almost,*
almost, yet find they slide by
like bright fantailed fish, all
but this one almost too near to see,

this one that offers us nothing
but this deep stirring of currents,
this hunger for stories woven of goods
borrowed or stolen from time. This one
that seems so tame until touched.

Dorothy Howe Brooks on "Weavings"

"Weavings" explores the *why* of poetry and art. A question without answers.
Yet this "absence of answers," paradoxically, is what drives the artist, the
poet, the musician. And the "weavings" that result, that come from the "deep
stirring of currents," turn out to be the very fabric, the "goods borrowed or
stolen," that "we" are made from. A remarkable insight, and one that

somehow plumbs the inexpressible depth that art takes us to, a notion "so tame until touched."

The language in this poem conveys the yearning that becomes the need to write. Its effective use of repetition—"of tea leaves, of stars, of" *or* "this one . . . this one . . . this one" *or, especially*, "woven of goods / borrowed or stolen"—enacts the very weaving that is the poem's theme.

Dorothy Howe Brooks

Late at Night, Waiting for My Son to Come Home

The thing that can't be said. The dread.

Shadows grow large as night comes on. Stillness slips through the windows, settles over the room, the city. Absence grows larger, grows heavy. Too heavy to bear. Stillness, shadows. And waiting.

The phone ringing. 4 a.m. Ringing. Ringing. Like a feral cat.

The man on the high wire sways in the breeze. Below, the falls. The boy swimming, sharks in the water. The child at the zoo slips from his mother's arms. The wolves.

Storm shutters are up. Life jackets fastened. Sirens. Clouds on the horizon.

Waiting, listening. For voices. For the sound of a car. For a door slamming. Then the ringing.

Not the storm but the cloud, black as an abyss,

bigger than the sky.

Dorothy Howe Brooks on "Late at Night, Waiting for My Son to Come Home"

I heard once that we often write about what we are most afraid of, and that is certainly true here. All those things we do to keep our children safe. All the terror. It is also true that I couldn't write this poem until my sons were safely beyond high school, which explains the reference to the telephone "ringing"—before the days of cell phones and constant contact!

I also wrote it, however, to experiment with the form—a form inspired by some poems by Laura Kasischke, whose work I greatly admire, in which

Kasischke sets the scene in the title, and the poem is simply related fragments and images gathered into short paragraphs. Such a form seemed exactly right for this poem.

Kerry Trautman on "Late at Night, Waiting for My Son to Come Home"

In her poem "Late at Night, Waiting for My Son to Come Home," Dorothy Howe Brooks deftly manipulates the pace of the reader's thoughts and breaths to pull us into the scene of the poem. It begins curtly: "The thing that can't be said. The dread." This unnamed thing just *is*, hovering there at the beginning of the poem, the matter of fact upon which the rest of the poem now hinges. The second stanza, with its long, wrapped lines, arrives in a whoosh, like a door blown open by a gust of wind, scattering papers about. Then the third stanza pokes again with its simple statements: "The phone ringing. 4 a.m. Ringing. Ringing." Pulsing, repeating like the ringing itself.

The unsettling images of stanzas four and five flow past, again with long lines that inhibit the reader's ability to pause, to fully examine one image before being thrust into the next—a rhythm that mimics the panicked thoughts in the parental mind. In the sixth stanza, we're delivered from the imaginary back to the physical surroundings of the poem's scene, with brief, simple phrases, as if we're trying to catch our breaths after a sprint. The final two lines, each given its own stanza, finally slow down, the breath steadying, bracing itself for what might come next.

Kerry Trautman

To the Iris

I had not anticipated how
you would dissolve yourselves—
your upward standard petals
collapsing and congealing,
dripping violet ooze onto the bureau top.
Such dramatic gore,
unlike other flowers' demure
beige wilting—
their slow fade until one day
I realize what I have displayed
in a tall glass vase now
is death, is yesterday, is
what-used-to-be
atop woody spindle stems.
But not you,
liquifying yourselves
to a resentful purple glop,
perhaps seeking my apologies for
clipping your succulent high stems
when your falls were at their zenith,
were spread to spring's spare sun,
beckoning bees to
your bearded, veined convolutions.
You will not go gently.

Kerry Trautman on "To the Iris"

All spring and into the summer, I clip flowers from the yard and bring them in. There's a large vase on the kitchen table and a small bud vase—made of green glass, a wedding gift—on the bathroom counter. I enjoy a rotating mish-mash of blossoms—whatever's blooming each time I stalk the yard with clippers.

My iris patch came from two neighbors whose own patches needed dividing. They planted the rhizomes along the east side of my house one October while I rested inside—very pregnant—and I didn't know until the following spring which colors they had planted.

That first spring I clipped some bright purple irises, and I brought the large vase to my bedroom. Purple is my favorite. I had no idea how quickly they would die. The buds would open, bloom a day or two, then dissolve like cotton candy drizzled with water. I had never seen flowers behave that way. As though they were angry. Or like toddlers throwing themselves limply to the floor to protest being told where to go. I suppose the poem was a sort of apology.

Rebecca Macijeski on "To the Iris"

There's a sense of inevitability and ephemerality in the way Kerry Trautman writes about the slow demise of her subject in "To the Iris." The blooms maintain their beauty and dignity even after "collapsing and congealing" into "a resentful purple glop." Trautman's irises die in a way that prolongs their story; they go out with a bang rather than the whimper of "other flowers' demure / beige wilting." They riot to their last moment, and Trautman witnesses the "dramatic gore" they leave on the bureau with an appreciation and care that grows into reverence. I'll admit that part of my love for this poem comes from the childhood nostalgia it brings out for me. Irises are my mother's favorite flower. Growing up in a small New England town, my siblings and I would measure the coming spring by when those proud purple blooms would shoot up along the driveway. Nearby were the lilac bushes whose flowers I would harvest for perfume as a girl, not knowing the way those small, purple stars would dissolve. Trautman's "violet ooze" brings me right back to that memory of discovering the exquisite decay of flowers, as well as the reminder that comes with it to appreciate the purple in them as it passes.

Rebecca Macijeski

Evening Market

Death is a woman this time,
and dying has never been more meticulous
in her hands. She walks through the market,
her heels a steady rhythm
on the pavement, a shadow among the colors,
collecting things. The ripe tomatoes
heavy with juice. The aroma of peaches
singing into the air. The beeping of the meat trucks
backing up to unload their sides of lamb,
pigeons scattering for seeds between the stalls.
She sees the big metallic fish lined up on ice,
gashed at the neck,
their gills flared open
like petticoats.
She sees the impeccable teeth
in the mouths of the fish.

Walking home, she watches the clouds
yellow out between the church spires,
the last of the sunlight
rounding along the vegetables.
Before long she'll be frying a trout whole
in a thin pool of butter, lemon juice sputtering
in the pan, setting the fish atop a bed of rice,
setting the table, steadying herself into a chair,
guiding her skirt as she sits,
using a knife and fork and her slight fingers
to remove and pile the tiny bones.

Rebecca Macijeski on "Evening Market"

The idea for the sequence begun by this poem was partially sparked by my reading of a Charles Simic poem. In his poem, Simic imagines Death's wife. I was intrigued by the notion of Death living a domestic life but wanted to take it further. What if Death was, herself, a woman? How might I color some of my own experiences and associations through her eyes? I wanted to show a version of Death who is like me—playful, observational, deeply curious, and introspective about what surrounds her. How wonderful, too, to think of Death not as fixated on the ends of things but interested instead in beginnings. In this way, Death can be a figure who teaches us about how to live, how to luxuriate in daily beauties as they present themselves to us. The scene of the poem also sweeps up images from a few key memories of mine—a transformative trout dinner and the many times I wandered through Boston's Haymarket awash in sounds and colors. There's nothing quite as sensorily rich for me as a street market toward the end of the day, with its various hums and ripenings.

Rachel Jamison Webster on "Evening Market"

Sometimes I think of the poetic as a shimmery realm that opens ordinary days into their own reflections—of the archetypal; of the world of dreams, fairy tales, and portents. This feeling of repetition sometimes occurs through sound and image, sometimes through a sense of recognition. I love "Evening Market" because it—and its author Rebecca Macijeski— know this realm. The poem gives us the lush abundance of a farmer's market, yet underlying all that autumnal life is death—as a woman, meticulously choosing and disembodying the fruits of life. The poem suggests that death's feminine presence, her appreciation of life's bounty and her inevitable selection from it, are the mortal forces that animate life's abundance. I can see "her slight fingers" that "remove and pile the tiny bones" and can understand that this is both a real woman—cooking, eating, and living—and death herself, taking care in her precise dismantling of matter. The fact that death is a woman "this time" also suggests that death, like life, takes on endless, and endlessly wondrous, forms.

Rachel Jamison Webster

NOBODY

One of my prized possessions
has long been lost.
It was a tiny photograph
I found at an antique shop,
among the cabinet cards of girls
in communion's white gauze,
those foggy faced, flower-boughed
ushers of the aughts.
It was a little square shot
of a girl in a bob, lovely,
with clear eyes and an impish gaze,
holding a sign in front of her unflawed face
on which someone had written
in capital letters NOBODY.
I looked into her eyes and decided
it was her own joke, the way a joke
is a form of knowing, as if she knew
the moment a hundred years later
when another girl in a bob would pluck it up
quickly, pay the fifty cents for it,
her hands almost shaking, almost hiding it
from the friends she was with.
Originality is so difficult to find.

In my own picture of that time—
a black and white strip
from a photo booth in a bar—
I am not at home in my skin,
but skittering its surfaces.
"There's something in you
you're not ready to admit to,"
John says when he sees it, and it's true

it will be years before I can
sit still before a camera or a man.
It will not happen until that smooth
beauty is gone, admitted to
as something lost. Her, too,
that NOBODY, is a ruse
because she is somebody
to the few who stand outside the frame
confused or laughing while she's
slipped through the joke to its truth,
the moment to its future, the
nobody she'll be in the next century,
seeing her clearly. Her truth
was to stare beyond the whole
sugar-drunk carnival of youth
and over the cardboard edge
of mortality. It was there
that she saw and was seen.

Rachel Jamison Webster on "NOBODY"

I have always loved the old photographs that I find in thrift shops and
antique stores. I'm haunted by the awareness that these infants, brides and
grooms, or little girls in communion dresses are no longer alive but were once
as real as you or me. You can look at your hand lifting up that old
photograph, or "cabinet card" as they were called, and it can appear as
ghostly, as unlikely, as their earnest faces, their hats trimmed with silk flowers
and satin. The most playful—and somehow the truest—of these photos that I
ever found was of a beautiful young girl who wore a dunce cap and held a
sign over her forehead that read "NOBODY." I imagined she had taken it at
some sort of carnival or circus, and I saw something profound in her smile.
She had the courage—disguised as flirty insouciance—to look down through
time into her own anonymity. For years I kept it close, meaning to get it
matted and framed, and I think I did get a mat for it, but then somehow I lost
it. It was just gone. It is often this way with sacred and mysterious things, it
seems, as if they are meant to be seen but not held. She was like that, too—a

beautiful young woman who knew that she wasn't to be held there, wasn't going to be misunderstood as only belonging to that story, that moment, that life. It sounds mystical, but when I think of the girl I was when I found that photo—twenty-two, lovely but very nervous and self-conscious, captured in a similarly compact photo strip—I know it's true. She doesn't exist anymore; she became someone else, who is me for a time, until I become what that girl knew all along: nobody.

The Editors on "NOBODY"

"NOBODY" speaks through its transcendence of time. I have always been fascinated by the idea that the past can survive in the form of tangible objects like photographs, and, to me, those photographs are very much like a window into another world. Rachel Jamison Webster captures this idea perfectly. In this poem, her narrator discovers a photograph that catches her interest, and she is intrigued, as the reader must be, by the "little square shot / of a girl in a bob, lovely, / with clear eyes and an impish gaze," holding a funny, horrifying, and deeply self-aware sign. Beyond our fascination, and the narrator's, lies a deeper truth: The girl in the photograph seems aware that her picture may live on, but she most certainly will not. Her self-awareness manifests as a gag; her "joke / is a form of knowing." "Nobody" in this picture will be remembered long after the girl herself is gone. (-*Katie Riddle*)

Luke Johnson

Chopping

An axe is a dream for idle boys.
Summer nights much easier

for these six or seven, alternating
unpracticed arcs, each heaving his

young weight and inexplicable blade
awkward into the honeylocust

planted between apartment stoops
and subway stops. A bike bolted

to the trunk: the only calculable target
for this aggression or revolution or willful

purposelessness. They want to chop
it down. They want to swing and swing

and swing, watch green underbark
give way to heartwood.

Bodies sweating under streetlamps.
When the tree falls, it's anti-climax,

slumping to the sidewalk like a man
who's had too much to drink, or

who's just tired of the same buildings
on the same walk in the same city.

Luke Johnson on "Chopping"

I wrote the poem "Chopping" after watching a YouTube video of a group of boys chopping down a tree in New York City. The video was taken by a surveillance camera, and these boys somehow got their hands on a genuine woodsman's ax. Even so, they were clearly not used to the work, and so the video spans over an hour, and several different young men take a turn on the handle. I watched the time-lapse, and I wondered why I was watching the video at all—if it was really so different from the reason they were chopping down the tree: to see something novel, to feel some small wrinkle in an otherwise unremarkable day, to avoid meaningful self-reflection. Once they'd finally worked through the trunk, the tree slumped over. There was no tremendous crash. The video had no sound. The boys watched the tree fall, and then they walked out of the frame.

The Editors on "Chopping"

Reading Luke Johnson's "Chopping," I am struck by the skill with which he captures youthful masculinity. The poem has an air of adolescent nostalgia that anyone who has been in the throes of boyhood will find impossible to resist. In fact, I vividly recall my own awkward attempts to hack at stumps, saplings, anything I could find on which to enact my desire to destroy. Such is the great strength of the poem. Johnson clearly pays attention to his diction: Each word here is as precise as the young boys' swings are *im*precise. The effect of this accuracy is twofold: It creates a tonal choppiness (a sort of nod to the subject of the poem?) and sets forth a clear path from beginning to end. The reader never loses himself in the margins of the poem; rather, he is immersed in the quick and simple action of the story. (-*Christian Mack*)

Biographical Notes

Lisa Dominguez Abraham teaches at Cosumnes River College. Her work has been published in journals such as *North American Review*, *Poetry East*, and the *Sacramento Voices* anthology, and her collection *Mata Hari Blows a Kiss* won the 2016 Swan Scythe Chapbook Contest.

Emily Allen teaches English and creative writing at the Louisiana School for Math, Science, and Arts in Natchitoches, Louisiana. She holds a Ph.D. in creative writing from the University of North Texas, and her work has previously appeared in *Prism*, *Eastern Iowa Review*, and *Barely South Review*. She is the faculty editor of *Its Lit*, a literary magazine for high school-aged writers.

Bruce Bond is the author of fifteen books, including, most recently, *For the Lost Cathedral* (LSU, 2015), *The Other Sky* (Etruscan, 2015), and *Immanent Distance: Poetry and the Metaphysics of the Near at Hand* (University of Michigan Press, 2015). Four of his books are forthcoming: *Black Anthem* (Tampa Review Prize, University of Tampa Press), *Gold Bee* (Crab Orchard Open Competition Award, Southern Illinois University Press), *Sacrum* (Four Way Books), and *Blackout Starlight: New and Selected Poems* (LSU). He is Regents Professor at University of North Texas.

Dorothy Howe Brooks writes poetry and fiction. Her work has appeared or is forthcoming in numerous literary journals, including *Atlanta Review*, *Poet Lore*, *Louisiana Literature*, *Bayou*, *Poem*, and *Mangrove Review*. Her second chapbook, *Interstices*, was published by Finishing Line Press, and her first full-length poetry collection, *A Fine Dusting of Brightness*, was published in 2013 by Aldrich Press.

Lauren Camp is the author of three books, most recently *One Hundred Hungers* (Tupelo Press, 2016), which won the Dorset Prize. Her poems have appeared in *New England Review*, *Poetry International*, *Slice*, *The Seattle Review*, *World Literature Today*, *Beloit Poetry Journal*, and other magazines. Her other literary honors include the Margaret Randall Poetry Prize, an Anna Davidson Rosenberg Award, and a Black Earth Institute Fellowship.

George David Clark is Assistant Professor of English at Washington & Jefferson College. His first book, *Reveille* (Arkansas, 2015), won the Miller Williams Prize, and more recent work can be found in *AGNI*, *The Cincinnati Review*, *The Gettysburg Review*, *Image*, *Third Coast*, and elsewhere. He edits the journal *32 Poems* and lives with his wife and their three young children in Washington, Pennsylvania.

Grant Clauser is the author of four books of poetry: *Reckless Constellations* (winner of the *Cider Press Review* Book Award), *The Magician's Handbook* (PS Books), *Necessary Myths* (Broadkill River Press) and *The Trouble with Rivers* (Foothills Publishing). His poems have appeared in *The American Poetry Review*, *Gargoyle*, *Painted Bride Quarterly*, *Southern Poetry Review*, *Tar River Poetry*, and other journals. He also writes about electronics and teaches in the Rosemont College Writers' Studio.

Kevin L. Cole has contributed poems to *The Briar Cliff Review*, *Paddlefish*, *Poetry East*, and other journals and has published one book of poetry: *Late Summer Plums*. He has received two South Dakota Arts Council/NEA grants: one for short fiction and one for poetry. He lives in and works in and around Sioux Falls, South Dakota.

Todd Davis is the author of five books of poems, most recently *Winterkill* and *In the Kingdom of the Ditch*, both published by Michigan State University Press. He is the editor of *Fast Break to Line Break: Poets on the Art of Basketball* (MSU Press, 2012) and *Making Poems: Forty Poems with Commentary by the Poets* (SUNY Press, 2010).

Joanne Diaz is Associate Professor of English at Illinois Wesleyan University and the author of two poetry collections: *My Favorite Tyrants* and *The Lessons*. With Ian Morris, she is the co-editor of *The Little Magazine in Contemporary America*. She is the recipient of fellowships from the Illinois Arts Council, the National Endowment for the Arts, the Bread Loaf Writers' Conference, and the Sustainable Arts Foundation.

Melissa Dickson is a poet and mother of four. Her work has appeared in *Shenandoah*, *North American Review*, *Southern Humanities Review*, *Literary Mama*, *Fickle Muses*, and *Southern Women's Review*. Her debut collection, *Cameo*, is available at Amazon.com, as are her Medusa-themed poems, collected under the title *Sweet Aegis*. She holds an MFA in Visual Arts from SVA and an MFA in poetry from Converse College.

Renee Emerson is the author of *Threshing Floor* (Jacar Press, 2016) and of *Keeping Me Still* (Winter Goose Publishing, 2014), a finalist for the Jacar Press Julie Suk Award for Best Poetry Book Published by an Independent Press in 2014. She currently resides in Arkansas with her husband and daughters.

Kerry James Evans is the author of *Bangalore* (Copper Canyon Press) and the recipient of a 2015 NEA fellowship. He lives and works in St. Louis, Missouri.

Amy Fant's work has appeared in *Driftwood Press*, *Weave Magazine*, *Nashville Review*, *The Kentucky Review*, and *Pulp Literature*, among other journals. Originally from South Carolina, she finished her MFA at Emerson College in Boston and is currently writing and teaching in Nashville, Tennessee.

Meg Freitag was born in Maine. She has a BA from Sarah Lawrence College and an MFA from UT Austin's Michener Center for Writers. Her work has appeared in *Tin House*, *Black Warrior Review*, and *Indiana Review*, among other journals. Her first book, *Edith*, was selected by Dorianne Laux as the winner of the 2016 BOAAT Book Prize and was published by BOAAT Press in fall 2017. She currently lives in the Bay Area.

Patricia L. Hamilton is a professor of English at Union University in Jackson, Tennessee. Her first volume of poetry, *The Distance to Nightfall*, was published in 2014 by Main Street Rag Press. Her most recent work has appeared in *Broad River Review*, *Third Wednesday*, *Red River Review*, and *Plainsongs*. She won the 2015 Rash Award for Poetry and has recently received her third Pushcart nomination.

Ava Leavell Haymon was Poet Laureate of Louisiana, 2013-2015. Her poems have appeared in journals and chapbooks nationwide and in three collections from LSU Press—most recently, *Why the House Is Made of Gingerbread*. She won the *Louisiana Literature* Prize for Poetry in 2003, the L.E. Phillabaum Poetry Award for 2010, and the Mississippi Institute of Arts and Letters 2010 Award in Poetry. She is editor of the Barataria Poetry Series from LSU Press.

Scott T. Hutchison has contributed to *The Chattahoochee Review*, *The Georgia Review*, and *The Southern Review*. His new work is forthcoming in *Atlanta Review*, *Fourth River*, *Aethlon*, *The Carolina Quarterly*, and *Tar River Poetry*.

Luke Johnson is the author of *After the Ark*. His poems have appeared in *New England Review*, *Poetry Northwest*, *The Southern Review*, *The Threepenny Review*, and other journals. He is Poetry Editor at *storySouth* and lives in Nashville, Tennessee, where he is a high school English teacher.

Eleanor Kedney is the author of the chapbook *The Offering* (Liquid Light Press, 2016). Her poems have appeared in a number of U.S. and international journals and anthologies. She founded the Tucson branch of the New York-based Writers Studio and served as the director and the master class teacher.

Ann Lauinger has written two books of poetry: *Persuasions of Fall* (University of Utah Press, 2004), winner of the Agha Shahid Ali Prize in Poetry, and *Against Butterflies* (Little Red Tree Publishing, 2013). Her poems have appeared in *The Georgia Review*, *Southern Poetry Review*, and other journals and have been anthologized or featured in *The Bedford Introduction to Literature*, *Poetry Daily*, *Verse Daily*, and Martha Stewart Living Radio.

William Logan's new book of poetry, *Rift of Light* (Penguin), was published in the fall. A book of long essays on familiar poems, *Dickinson's Nerves, Frost's Woods* (Columbia University Press), will follow in April.

Richard Luftig is the author of three published chapbooks, a recipient of the Cincinnati Post-Corbett Foundation Award for Literature, and a semi-finalist for the Emily Dickinson Society Award. His poems have appeared in numerous national and international journals and have been translated into Japanese, Polish, German, and Finnish.

Rebecca Macijeski holds a Ph.D. from the University of Nebraska Lincoln and an MFA from Vermont College of Fine Arts. She has attended artists' residencies at The Ragdale Foundation, Art Farm Nebraska, and the Kimmel Harding Nelson Center and has served as poetry editor for *Prairie Schooner* and *Hunger Mountain*. Her poems have appeared in *The Missouri Review*, *The Journal*, *Nimrod*, *Poet Lore*, and other magazines. She is Assistant Professor at Northwestern State University.

Angie Macri is the author of *Underwater Panther* (Southeast Missouri State University), winner of the Cowles Poetry Book Prize, and *Fear Nothing of the Future or the Past* (Finishing Line). An Arkansas Arts Council fellow, she lives in Hot Springs.

Al Maginnes is the author of *The Next Place* and of six other collections. He has recent poems in *Mount Hope*, *Beyu*, and other journals. He lives in Raleigh, North Carolina, and teaches at Wake Technical Community College.

Shara McCallum is a Jamaican-American writer and the author of five books of poetry published in the U.S. and the U.K., most recently *Madwoman* (2017). Her work has been translated into several languages and has received such recognition as a Witter Bynner Fellowship from the Library of Congress and an NEA Poetry Fellowship. She lives in Pennsylvania and teaches creative writing and literature at Penn State University.

Davis McCombs is the author of two collections: *Ultima Thule* (Yale 2000), which was a finalist for the National Book Critics Circle Award, and *Dismal Rock* (Tupelo 2007), which won the Dorset Prize. He is currently the Director of the Creative Writing Program at the University of Arkansas in Fayetteville.

Matthew Minicucci is the author of two collections of poetry: *Translation* (Kent State University Press, 2015), chosen by Jane Hirshfield for the 2014 Wick Poetry Prize, and *Small Gods* (New Issues Press, 2017). His work has appeared in numerous journals and anthologies, including *Best New Poets 2014*, *Poetry Daily*, and *Verse Daily*, among others.

Julie L. Moore is the author of *Particular Scandals*, published in the Poiema Poetry Series by Cascade Books. Her other books include *Slipping Out of Bloom* (WordTech Editions), and *Election Day* (Finishing Line Press). She has contributed poetry to *Alaska Quarterly Review*, *Image*, *Nimrod*, *Poetry Daily*, *Prairie Schooner*, *The Southern Review*, *Verse Daily*, and other journals and anthologies.

Carolyn Oliver is a graduate of The Ohio State University and Boston University and lives in Massachusetts with her family. Her work is forthcoming in *The Worcester Review* and has appeared in *Day One*, *Tin House*'s "Open Bar," *Scoundrel Time*, *America: The Jesuit Review*, *matchbook*, and elsewhere.

Angie Crea O'Neal holds the Joan Alden Speidel Chair in English at Shorter University in Rome, Georgia, where she lives with her daughters. Her poems have appeared in *San Pedro River Review, Kindred, Gravel, Stirring: A Literary Collection*, and other journals. Her chapbook, *The Way Things Fall*, is available through Anchor & Plume Press.

April Ossmann is the author of *Anxious Music* (Four Way Books) and *Event Boundaries* (FWB) and a recipient of a 2013 Vermont Arts Council Creation Grant for a manuscript-in-progress.

Ricardo Pau-Llosa is the author of seven books of poetry; the latest, *Man*, published in 2014 by Carnegie Mellon U. Press, is his fifth title with the Press. He has new and forthcoming appearances in *The Hudson Review, december, The American Poetry Review, Stand, Plume*, and other literary magazines. He is also an art critic and curator.

Doug Ramspeck is the author of six poetry collections and one collection of short stories. His most recent book, *Black Flowers*, is forthcoming from LSU Press. Individual poems have appeared in *The Kenyon Review, Slate, The Georgia Review, The Southern Review*, and many other journals.

Bobby C. Rogers is Professor of English and Writer-in-Residence at Union University. His first book, *Paper Anniversary*, won the Agnes Lynch Starrett Poetry Prize. In 2015, he was named a Witter Bynner Fellow at the Library of Congress by Poet Laureate Charles Wright. His new book, *Social History*, has just been released by LSU Press in their Southern Messenger Poets series.

Jay Rogoff has published six books of poems, most recently *Enamel Eyes, A Fantasia on Paris, 1870* (2016), *Venera* (2014), *The Art of Gravity* (2011), and *The Long Fault* (2008), all published by LSU Press. His work appears in many journals, including *The Hudson Review, Literary Imagination, The Southern Review, Salmagundi*, and *The Hopkins Review*, where he serves as dance critic. He lives in Saratoga Springs, New York, where he teaches at Skidmore College.

M. S. Rooney lives in Sonoma, California, with her husband, the poet Dan Noreen. Her work has appeared in a number of journals, including *Bluestem, The Cortland Review, Earth's Daughters, Main Street Rag, Theodate*, and *3:AM*

Magazine, as well as several anthologies, including *American Society: What Poets See*, edited by David Chorlton and Robert S. King (FutureCycle Press), and *Journey to Crone*, edited by S. Philipp (Chuffed Buff Books).

Shane Seely is the author of two books of poems: *The Surface of the Lit World*, winner of the 2014 Hollis Summers Prize from Ohio University Press, and *The Snowbound House*, winner of the 2008 Philip Levine Prize for Poetry. His chapbook of poems, *History Here Requires Balboa*, was published by Slash Pine Press in 2012. He is an associate professor of English at the University of Missouri-St. Louis, where he teaches in the MFA program in creative writing.

Austin Segrest is a native Alabaman and teaches poetry in north-central Wisconsin. He holds a Ph.D. from the University of Missouri, where he studied Puritans, among other things, and was poetry editor of *The Missouri Review*. His poems can be found in *The Threepenny Review*, *The Yale Review*, *Blackbird*, *Ploughshares*, *Image*, and *Harvard Review*. He currently reviews poetry for *Southern Humanities Review*.

David Shattuck is a writing professor at Texas Woman's University. He received an MA from University of North Texas and an MFA from Eastern Washington University. He is the author of *Invisible Cities*, which was published by CW Books in September 2013.

Karissa Knox Sorrell is a poet and ESOL teacher from Nashville, Tennessee. She is the author of the chapbook *Evening Body* (Finishing Line Press, 2016) and a graduate of the Murray State University MFA program.

Marjorie Stelmach is the author of *Falter* (Cascade Books, 2017), as well as four other collections of poetry. Her work has recently appeared in *Boulevard*, *The Cincinnati Review*, *The Gettysburg Review*, *Image*, *The Iowa Review*, *New Letters*, and other journals.

Brian Swann is the author of the poetry collections *In Late Light* (Johns Hopkins University Press), *Sky Loom: Native American Myth, Story, Song* (University of Nebraska Press), *St. Francis and the Flies* (winner of the Autumn House Poetry Prize), and *Companion, Analogies* (Sheep Meadow Press), as well as the story collection *Dogs on the Roof* (MadHat Press).

Gail Thomas has published four books, and her work has appeared in many journals and anthologies, including *Beloit Poetry Journal*, *Calyx*, *North American Review*, and *Valparaiso Poetry Review*. Her chapbook *Odd Mercy* was chosen by Ellen Bass for the Charlotte Mew Prize of Headmistress Press, and *Waving Back* was named a "Must Read" for 2016 by the Massachusetts Center for the Book. Her other books are *No Simple Wilderness* and *Finding the Bear*.

Kerry Trautman has contributed to *The Toledo Review*, *Alimentum*, *Coe Review*, *Third Wednesday*, and *Think Journal*, as well as to anthologies, including *Tuesday Night at Sam and Andy's Uptown Café* (Westron Press, 2001), *Mourning Sickness* (Omniarts, 2008), and *Roll* (Telling Our Stories Press, 2012).

Chase Twichell is the author, most recently, of *Horses Where the Answers Should Have Been: New & Selected Poems* (Copper Canyon 2010), which won both the Kingsley Tufts Award from Claremont Graduate University and the Balcones Poetry Prize. She splits the year between the Adirondacks and Miami Beach.

Jeanne Murray Walker has published eight collections of poetry, including, most recently, *Helping the Morning: New and Selected Poems* (Word Farm Press, 2014). Her award-winning plays have been produced around the U.S. and in London. Her memoir, *The Geography of Memory: A Pilgrimage through Alzheimer's*, was published in 2013 by Hachette Press, and in 2015 she co-edited with Luci Shaw *Ambition: Essays by Members of The Chrysostom Society*.

Rachel Jamison Webster directs the Creative Writing Program at Northwestern University. She is author of the books *September* and *The Endless Unbegun*, and her poems and essays have appeared in many journals and anthologies, including *Tin House*, *Poetry*, *The Paris Review*, and *Narrative*.

Karen J. Weyant has contributed poetry and prose to *Barn Owl Review*, *Caesura*, *Cold Mountain Review*, *Poetry East*, *River Styx*, *Waccamaw*, and *Whiskey Island*. Her most recent collection of poetry, *Wearing Heels in the Rust Belt*, won Main Street Rag's 2011 chapbook contest and was published in 2012. She teaches at Jamestown Community College in Jamestown, New York.

Acknowledgements

The Cumberland River Review wishes to acknowledge and thank all of the editors who have contributed to its first five years (managing editors in bold text):

Noula Arroyo	Marina Asaad	Katerine Avila-Pastor
Devon Babcock	Elizabeth Baxter	Fallon Bechtel
Jonathan Brooks	Layton Byrd	**Justin Cockrell**
Grayson Dance	Katie Dickau	Emily Diehl
Taylor Dowd	Joshua Flatt	Katrina Ford
Torri Frye	Deborah Givens	Jon Grimo
Korey Grohler	Virginia Hensley	Jeff Hopkins
Amanda Johnson	Dillon Jones	**Christian Keen**
Aaron Joel Lain	Jackson Lawrence	Kim Lilienthal
Christian Mack	**Crystal Martel**	Kaitlyn Mays
Erin Miller	James Abram Miller	**Todd Osborne**
Andrew Raney	Katie Riddle	Amy Taylor
Jordan Taylor	Jessy Walters	Abbi Watkins
Tori White	**Erin Wiese**	

Made in the USA
Columbia, SC
29 January 2021